SEX, TOURISM AND THE
POSTCOLONIAL ENCOUNTER

New Directions in Tourism Analysis

Series Editor: Dimitri Ioannides, E-TOUR, Mid Sweden University, Sweden

Although tourism is becoming increasingly popular as both a taught subject and an area for empirical investigation, the theoretical underpinnings of many approaches have tended to be eclectic and somewhat underdeveloped. However, recent developments indicate that the field of tourism studies is beginning to develop in a more theoretically informed manner, but this has not yet been matched by current publications.

The aim of this series is to fill this gap with high quality monographs or edited collections that seek to develop tourism analysis at both theoretical and substantive levels using approaches which are broadly derived from allied social science disciplines such as Sociology, Social Anthropology, Human and Social Geography, and Cultural Studies. As tourism studies covers a wide range of activities and sub fields, certain areas such as Hospitality Management and Business, which are already well provided for, would be excluded. The series will therefore fill a gap in the current overall pattern of publication.

Suggested themes to be covered by the series, either singly or in combination, include – consumption; cultural change; development; gender; globalisation; political economy; social theory; sustainability.

Also in the series

A Planner's Encounter with Complexity
Edited by Gert de Roo and Elisabete A. Silva
ISBN 978-1-4094-0265-7

Development Tourism
Lessons from Cuba
Rochelle Spencer
ISBN 978-0-7546-7542-6

Sex Tourism in Africa
Kenya's Booming Industry
Wanjohi Kibicho
ISBN 978-0-7546-7460-3

Cultures of Mass Tourism
Doing the Mediterranean in the Age of Banal Mobilities
Edited by Pau Obrador Pons, Mike Crang and Penny Travlou
ISBN 978-0-7546-7213-5

Sex, Tourism and the Postcolonial Encounter
Landscapes of Longing in Egypt

JESSICA JACOBS
Royal Holloway, University of London, UK

Routledge
Taylor & Francis Group

LONDON AND NEW YORK

First published 2010 by Ashgate Publishing

Published 2016 by Routledge
2 Park Square, Milton Park, Abingdon, Oxfordshire OX14 4RN
711 Third Avenue, New York, NY 10017, USA

First issued in paperback 2016

Routledge is an imprint of the Taylor & Francis Group, an informa business

British Library Cataloguing in Publication Data
Jacobs, Jessica.
  Sex, tourism and the postcolonial encounter : landscapes of
  longing in Egypt. -- (Gender, ethnicity and power in
  tourism)
  1. Culture and tourism--Egypt--Sinai. 2. Women
  travelers--Egypt--Sinai--Attitudes. 3. Women travelers--
  Sexual behavior--Egypt--Sinai. 4. Sex tourism--Egypt--
  Sinai. 5. Sinai (Egypt)--Social conditions--21st century.
  I. Title II. Series
  306.4'819'09531-dc22

Library of Congress Cataloging-in-Publication Data
Jacobs, Jessica, 1965-
  Sex, tourism and the postcolonial encounter : landscapes of longing in Egypt / by Jessica Jacobs.
    p. cm. -- (New directions in tourism analysis)
  Includes bibliographical references and index.
  ISBN 978-0-7546-4788-1 (hardback) -- ISBN 978-0-7546-8904-1 (ebook)
  1. Sex tourism--Egypt. 2. Tourists--Sexual behavior--Egypt. 3. Women travelers--Sexual behavior--Egypt. 4. Egypt--Social conditions. I. Title.

  HQ445.E3J33 2010
  306.74'309531--dc22

                                                                    2010022182

ISBN 13: 978-1-138-25014-7 (pbk)
ISBN 13: 978-0-7546-4788-1 (hbk)

Contents

For Liselott, Safi and Suraya

List of Figures

Preface

... doesn't everybody travel so as to fall in love? – whether it be with a woman
or a man or with a whole people – with their cities, their landscapes, their music,
their cooking, their children, their hunger for justice – or even with their hunger?
Milton Friedman's Smile: Travel and Culture and the Poetics of a City (Osborne
1990).

Sex tourism is supposed to match geographically ascribed gender identities of inequality between the West and the global South where the West is often positioned as masculine, a colonial and neoliberal force that 'penetrates' the 'feminised' land and people of the global South, exploiting and holding them in its 'male' (Mulvey 1975) or 'tourist' (Urry 1990) gaze. Other hegemonies, within race and ethnicity, position whiteness in a masculinised and powerful role, with the non-white person feminised and powerless.

But what happens to these gendered and racial global discourses of power when they are applied to other forms of tourist–local relationships? What happens when the 'sex tourist' is a woman who travels to engage in relationships with 'local' men?[1]

Is it even sex tourism? Certainly 'ethnosexual relationships' (Nagel 2003) between tourist women and local men, if they are considered at all, are generally considered to be a sub-category of the more widespread practice of Western male sex tourism. Yet this subsumption is not always that straightforward. For example, in 2008 the British journalist Diana Appleyard wrote an article about British women who holidayed in Turkey, Egypt, Jamaica, the Gambia and Kenya[2] for the UK's *Daily Mail* newspaper. The article, 'Sun, sand, sex and stupidity: Why thousands of middle-aged women are obsessed with holiday gigolos', described women who travel for sex as middle-aged and generally unattractive. So far, so like the male sex tourist stereotype. However the article concludes these women are also 'stupid' because they are being 'ripped-off' by the men who are only engaging in sex for economic benefit. This is very different to assumptions about the male sex tourist who is supposedly clearly involved in a financial exchange, is generally considered to be in control of this exchange and whose behaviour is not seen to contradict expectations surrounding masculine identities.

---

1   Although the men are thought of as local and this is an important part of their appeal as I will argue later, 'local' men have often travelled to tourist resorts from elsewhere in the same or a neighbouring country.

2   Appleyard (2008) 'Sun, sand, sex and stupidity: Why thousands of middle-aged women are obsessed with holiday gigolos', *Daily Mail*.

Perhaps what is more interesting however, is that alongside this article are photographic stills from *Vers la Sud* (*Heading South*) (dir. Laurent Cantent 2005) starring Charlotte Rampling and *Shirley Valentine* (dir. Lewis Gilbert 1989). Unlike the text, these two films present the female sex tourist in much more glamorous and positive terms. These films, and others such as the Caribbean-based *How Stella Got Her Groove Back* (dir. Kevin Rodney Sullivan 1998), portray female 'sex' tourists as attractive women who are escaping from oppressive relationships in their own society and searching for sexual freedom.

Sex Tourism or Romance Tourism?

The sexual relationships that occur between tourist women and local men in the holiday hotspots of the South are clearly more diverse and complex than these stereotypical representations would suggest.

Women's sexual tourism first came to academic attention in the 1970s when the introduction of package holidays and charter flights enabled women in Europe and North America to travel alone in far greater numbers. To date studies on this kind of tourism have tended to focus on the Caribbean and Central America, in particular the tropical beach resort, now synonymous with the gendered mass tourism experience first described by Wagner (1977) in Gambia. Although other beach resorts in West Africa, Indonesia (Dahles and Bras 1999), and Israel (Cohen 1971) have also been explored as well as other landscapes, such as Jerusalem's Old City (Bowman 1996), the main question asked about these women tends to be: 'Are they or aren't they like male sex tourists?' Phillips (1999: 183), for example, describes this activity, commonly referred to as 'female sex tourism', as a racial and gendered 'quest', 'where the white emancipated Western female goes in search of the quintessential hypersexual black male in the center of the Other'. O'Connell Davidson and Sanchez Taylor's (1999) survey of 104 single Western female tourists in the Caribbean concludes that, like Western men, they were engaging in relationships of exploitation:

> Like their male counterparts Western female sex tourists employ fantasies of Otherness not just to legitimate obtaining sexual access to the kind of young, fit, handsome bodies that would otherwise be denied to them and to obtain affirmation of their own sexual desirability but also to obtain a sense of power and control over themselves and others as engendered, sexual beings and to affirm their own privilege as Westerners (O'Connell Davidson and Sanchez Taylor 1999, 49).

In contrast, Pruitt and LaFont (1995) and others (such as Dahles and Bras 1999) argue that Western heterosexual women are different because there is an emotional element to these sexual relationships. Therefore these encounters are better defined as 'romance tourism', 'where the actors place emphasis on courtship rather than the exchange for money and sex' (Pruitt and LaFont 1995: 243).

This tendency to position women's ethnosexual relationships with local men within the context of male sex tourism has, I would argue, led to constrictive, circular research, that as Jeffreys (2003) notes, fails to take into account the different class–sex positions of men and women and even more problematically threatens to legitimise prostitution as harmless fun. It also positions women as secondary to (and imitative of) men and confines research into this subject to spheres already marked out by work on male sex tourism, such as sex and money. By highlighting the racialised and economically disparate nature of these exchanges the importance of imaginative and emotional geographies caught up in such relationships are, for the most part, being ignored. Furthermore the paradigm of exploitation does not get analysed sufficiently and it does not give enough room to examine the ambiguities and interactions of the power lines of gender and race that are raised by such encounters. It also tends to ignore the spatial and temporal; especially concerning the colonial historical relationships between host and guest and the specificity of the beach/paradise location.

This book does not dispute that Western (mostly white) women who sleep with local men in the tourist resorts of the South exploit their First World and racial privileges in their search for a sexualised and racialised 'other'. Neither does it deny that women often construct and perform these relationships with reference to narratives of romance. However it will argue that these tourist encounters, when defined as 'sex tourism', are often presented within over-simplified binaries of gender and race (white women exploiting black men); while its alternative 'romance tourism' uses romance too narrowly, normally to refer solely to an essentialised idea of Western femininity.

The search to find – and sleep with – a 'hypersexual', racial other is not that straightforward, nor is it the only search. Geographical imaginaries and emotions involved with conceptions of distance, time and landscape (to name a few aside from sex) – and their relationship to the men they get involved with, are also an integral component in the attraction, performance and effect of such relationships. Romance yes, and emotional involvement, but for many women who go on holiday and end up sleeping with local men, this 'journey' cannot be reduced to a romance with the 'other', or an exploitative encounter with an imagined essentialised masculinity. For many it is also a romance of time travel to locations deemed somehow to exist outside of their own time/modernity and this romance is certainly not exclusively reserved for the male objects of desire.

There are of course different histories of colonialism and race that make any direct comparison between women's relationships in the Caribbean and other tourist hotspots unhelpful. Nevertheless it is important to expand the current regional focus on the Caribbean to include female sex/romance tourism in destinations where racial distinctions are less clear, economic disparity is not always as extreme, and the beach is not the only landscape of attraction. In the Sinai tourist resorts of Egypt, where sexual encounters with 'local' men are a popular component of

Western women's holidays, the desert is often as alluring as the beach and men can be 'whiter' than their Western girlfriends, as well as wealthier.[3] And, as we shall see, not even 'local'. As Frohlick (2005: 10) says of the women who go to Costa Rica,

> ...it is not a simple matter of women coming to the Caribbean coast to necessarily seek out men, although that does of course happen...sexualities and sexualization unfolds in the tourist destination in contingent ways but arising from specific histories, power relations, and representational contexts.

Based on fieldwork interviews with men and women in the resorts of the South Sinai, Egypt, I will argue that these encounters can be seen as examples of a modern subjectivity that are defined by and take place within imagined (fixed) constructions of landscapes, native Third World masculinity (in this case Arab/ Bedouin), femininity (white, heterosexual, Western), freedom and love (spiritual and physical): all presented in some form of opposition to a particularist idea of modernity and viewed through a filter of selective (and spatially circumscribed) histories. By adding a geographical dimension to the debate on women's sexual travel, I aim to open up the current debate on female sex tourism to a wider range of issues and reveal more of the conflicts, tensions and imaginations that make up these encounters.

Time and Place

My fieldwork centred on the tourist resorts of the Sinai, Egypt. But what is it about the men in, and the resorts of, the Sinai that are so appealing to Western women? As we have seen female 'sex tourism' has been noted in several holiday destinations, most notably the Caribbean, but also other tropical beach resorts in countries with a reputation for a third-world masculinity.

These reputations of place and people can be traced to geographical imaginations that are crucial to the construction of holiday destinations and why one destination is chosen over another. The Orient has been a site of performance for European visitors since the days of the Empire (and beyond), geographically imagined as a stage for the enactment, as well as the dissemination of colonial practices and ideas. In contemporary tourism, the image-laden landscapes of Southwest Asia, the Eastern Mediterranean and North Africa are key selling points, particularly those that evoke historical–geographical imaginations of deserts, oases and ancient Islamic market focused cities. Orientalist masculinities are also key – stereotypical fantasies of the romantic Arab/Bedouin sheikh are reproduced everywhere in

---

3   It is not uncommon for middle and upper middle class Egyptians from Cairo and Alexandria to identify as 'white' in comparison with Upper Egyptians (Luxor, Aswan) and Africans in general.

Western society: in our films, our books, adverts, television programmes, even fashion magazine spreads. When it comes to choosing a holiday these images are even more condensed down to the core exotic values of the desert/Bedouin/palm tree motif in our travel brochures.

In Chapter 1, I will explore how these images within popular travel literature have been used to help to establish Western (masculine) notions of hegemony through its construction of the 'other' in the people and places of the Middle East.

Contemporary tourism is very much focused on 'getting away from it all', from the stresses and strains of modern life. The tourist and tourist marketing, with all the inherent contradictions that modernity can offer, has inherited and absorbed this legacy of Empire and often attempts to replicate nostalgic colonial geographical imaginations. Holidays offer the modern tourist the opportunity to 'retread' the steps of famous colonial travellers. But tourists, particularly women tourists, also want a suntan and authenticity. Like their Victorian predecessors they want to interact with the locals and 'understand' the culture. I will argue that when it comes to visiting the 'Orient' tourists are encouraged – and want – to experience it as a series of places that reference the colonial past.

In contemporary tourism the template for a sex tourist is a man from Western Europe or North America paying for sex with a woman from a developing country. In contrast women are largely viewed as advocates of the 'ethnic encounter'. In Chapter 2, I will argue that the notion of the ethnic encounter is, if not explicitly, then implicitly sexualised when it comes to Third World travel. In addition the gendered aspect of this form of travel borrows heavily from imaginations when intrepid women writers, artists and photographers ventured out into the colonies. Without recourse to professional status, gender has always been paramount in their profile. It has been suggested that because they were women they held an ambivalent position within the colonial project. Therefore they were more interested in, and likely to engage and identify with, natives. Today, Victorian women travel writers and photographers are viewed as feminist pioneers and referenced as role models by many contemporary women travellers.

In contrast to the dominant discourses of neoliberal politics, notions of authenticity and the valorisation of 'simple' native cultures tend to portray 'modern' Western society as inferior to the 'undeveloped' world in terms of spirituality, purity and proximity to 'nature'. However these values also rely upon opposing binaries that establish the tourist/Westerner as sovereign subject and 'otherise' the locals and landscapes they visit; through ideas of here and there, ancient and modern, civilised and wilderness, pure and corrupt, sophisticated and simple, cold and hot, frigid and erotic, etc. I argue that when this is applied to modern women's travel, this has led to the adoption and adaptation of modernity's masculinised mobility as an act of emancipation for women in the West while the fixed and travelled upon are still associated with a feminised sexual transgressiveness and a lack of modernity.

I have particularly selected to examine contradictions and apparent paradoxes that revolve around the supposed switching of stereotypes of expected behaviour of gender, race and modernity. These are often expressed in the form of binaried opposites such as male and female, black and white, first and Third World, East and West, but also other dichotomies that are formed around ideas of modernity and the modern subject, such as the tourer and the toured, the mobile and the fixed, ancient and modern and civilisation and wilderness.

The arguments presented here are based on fieldwork conducted in the Red Sea tourist resorts of the Sinai in 2002 when I conducted 57 interviews with (mostly white) heterosexual tourist women and local men, most of whom had (or were) engaged in sexual relationships.[4] While the paradise beach has long been associated with women's sexual tourism, the desert has not received much attention. In Chapter 3, I introduce the resorts of the Sinai and further explore the binaried constructions of place and gender, particularly those surrounding Arab masculinity and historicised desert landscapes. I argue that women tourists and travellers construct the Sinai *and* its men through an Orientalist geographical imagination. These imaginations include conceptualisations of the Sinai's holiday resorts with their hotels, beaches and swimming pools, as sites suitable for sex and a suntan and the Sinai's desert as a wilderness, an empty, marginal space suitable for getting closer to nature through sex. All locations on offer to the female tourist/traveller represent freedom and in many cases local men, seen to embody a condition of un- or pre- or anti-modernity, act as 'gatekeepers' so that entering into sexual or romantic relationships with local men allows the women to experience or consume these historicised landscapes of longing.

It is men's travel that has long been associated with freedom, especially sexual freedom and in Chapter 4 I will go on to look at the gendered association with travel and the modern subject, especially those involving these representations of paradise and the desert. I will go on to explore the role of mobility on these romantic sexual encounters in order to argue that these women set out to escape modernity but use modernity to achieve this. They exploit their privileged position and their mobility – they 'travel' in order to create an imaginary where the Sinai desert, and its population, represent Nature and Wilderness, a place of freedom not only on the margins of a modern Europe geographically, but historically, as a place perceived to exist in a time outside of our modernity.

This freedom however cannot always be taken for granted and it is rare for women's travel to be discussed without a focus on their supposed vulnerability as women, particularly concerning sexual threat. Despite attempts to control women's mobility it would seem that travelling, and the prospect of sex or romance

---

4   I carried out the interviews over four months (split into two month periods in the Spring and Autumn). My ethnographic fieldwork was augmented by several other visits to the area working for the *Rough Guide Egypt* in 1999 and 2002 and other visits. I have been visiting this region since 1985 and having prior knowledge of (some of) the people and places of my study definitely affected the interpretation of my data. All names have been changed.

when travelling, is becoming more and more relevant to Western women who are travelling in ever greater numbers, often alone.

While the main focus of this book is Western women, in particular those from Western Europe, Chapter 5 explores the issues dealt with in previous chapters from the perspective of the local men, looking at their geographical imaginations of both Europe (or the Occident) and the Sinai. If the men embody an anti-modernity for the women tourists these same women represent a form of modernity for the men who also incorporate racialised and sexualised stereotypes in their geographical imaginations of the West and Western European women, while often attempting to fulfil the women's stereotypes of them. By establishing (sexual/romantic) relationships in the 'modern' resorts of the Sinai many men gain access to this notion of modernity. The tensions and conflicts held within these opposing binaries of meaning can, of course, lead to problems but perhaps they can also result in a negotiation of modernity. The personal nature of these relationship and the women's (subordinate) gender means that they can certainly be beneficial to these men compared with say, relationships they might have with other (impersonal and inequitable) forms of modernity such as global capital.

All of these encounters between Western women and local men take place in and around tourist resorts. The tourist resort is a crucial site for the sexualised ethnic encounter as it offers place for performance and interaction not always available to women in Europe, or to the men in Cairo and the rest of Egypt. Such experimentation and reconstitution of identity and the negotiations of modernity between the couples takes place in tourist spaces of encounter – the tourist zone. These include a variety of different sites in the Sinai but all act as contemporary stages for performance of these identities by both tourist/traveller women and local men; stages where the meaning and content of modernity and gender and sexual identities are negotiated. In Chapter 6, I argue that tourist space can act as places to negotiate ideas of modernity, gender, race, and so on. Through binaries and travelling – experiencing otherness in a safe environment – the tourist resort becomes a mediated space.

Gendered power relations mean that the structure of global inequality isn't simply reproduced; there is a negotiation going on. Furthermore the tourist zone is crucial to the criss-crossing of power relations. It is a space for mediating concepts of modernity, gender and race/ethnicity. This occupation of a space of difference is caused by women with First World spending power and cultural capital, travelling and being 'out of time and place' (Wagner 1977). I conclude that it is the combination of First World privilege and geographical imaginations – the women's mobility and their stereotyping of the male inhabitants (an embodiment and expression of their ideas of modernity and its opposites) that allow for experimentation with, and reconstituting of, dominant narratives of sexual and other identities of both the female 'tourist/traveller' and the male local. Engaging in relationships with local men therefore, can be seen as way in to this condition, a way to express feelings of anti-modernity and to gain access to the landscape and culture of their geographical imaginations, a way to escape the perceived superficiality of the modern tourist experience. But this is no simple binary at work – there is more than one 'opposite' to modernity and these alternatives to modernity themselves 'travel'.

By taking a closer look at these 'opposites' and their embeddedness in Western imaginaries of paradise and deserts these women show they are not just having sex with a native, but the relationships they engage in are a means to 'travel' to these three overlapping and interconnected places and spaces of the 'un-modern', 'pre-modern' and 'anti-modern' – spaces that travel, and travel in different directions making a straightforward binary between the modern and its opposite unworkable and upsetting some of the dualistic essentialisms constructed around gender and the 'Third World'. The relationships that ensue therefore can only occur because the tourist resort acts as an intermediary space, where interaction between the women and men allow ideas of modernity to be negotiated through a gendered and racialised discourse.

Jessica Jacobs
June 2010

Acknowledgements

Firstly I would like to thank all the people who agreed to be interviewed during the course of my fieldwork in Egypt. Also, everyone at the Geography Department of the Open University, in particular Doreen Massey and Steve Pile. Professor Massey's insightful analysis and comments remain an inspiration for all my work and I am very grateful to her.

I would also like to mention Alexa Firat from Temple University in Philadelphia, Richard Phillips at the University of Liverpool and Umut Erel from the Open University for their support and encouragement. I am also grateful to my anonymous reviewers from the journal *Gender, Place and Culture* for their helpful comments and the editorial staff at Ashgate for their patience.

Chapter 1
Nostalgia for Travel – Adventure Travel and the Ethnic Encounter in Egypt

Introduction

The term 'geographical imaginations' was adopted by Gregory (1994) to refer to the ways in which social life is 'embedded in space, place and landscape'. When the term is applied to tourism and tourist practice it can be said to be a crucial element in determining the final choice of destination, because before we go anywhere for the first time on holiday we often have a strong idea of what it will be like. Indeed we choose one tourist destination over another because of how we imagine the social life of its space, place and landscape. But holiday-oriented geographical imaginations of place – what Löfgren (1999: 2) calls 'vacationscapes' – can sit uneasily when it comes to the holiday hotspots of the global South, where imaginations of exotic paradises peopled with colourful, traditional, friendly natives are also places of poverty, disease and despotism. Those who market these destinations understandably avoid mention of authoritarian rule, human rights abuse or the lack of access to good health facilities, clean water and education etc – unless it is aesthetically repackaged in a way that portrays local people as living a simple lifestyle devoid of all the hassles of modern day life. The tourist landscape is constructed, both literally in the shape of gated tourist resorts and theme parks, and symbolically through the geographical imaginations of tour operators and tourists.

Tourism seeks to capitalise on differences between places, often spatial and cultural in scope and as Momsen (1994: 129) notes, when this takes place in a developing country, tourism 'has all the elements of domination, exploitation and manipulation characteristic of colonialism'. With their links to what is often termed the largest global industry, 'vacationscapes' tend to dominate other more local geographical imaginations and, indeed, often only manage to maintain their hegemony (and income-generating properties) by denying localised geographical imaginations. Of course, a complete tourist 'bubble' (McCannell 1976, Judd 1999) is difficult to maintain, but intrusions can be explained away by tourists and the tourist industry through spatial and temporal discourses of difference such as Orientalism and the racial and sexual stereotyping of 'others' which often (but not always) juxtaposes the modern mobile 'First World' tourist against a 'Third World' local who is a fixed identity without agency.

The hegemony of the tourist imaginary enables the tourist to enjoy his or her paradise. The tourist imaginary does more than blot out unwelcome thoughts of disparity – it constructs Third World destinations as ancient, timeless, immobile places populated by people who somehow manage to exist outside modernity.

Contemporary tourism however is not just a modern form of colonialism as Momsen argues, it is also a re-enactment or a return to the historical period when tourism was first established as part of modern Western culture, and nowhere is this more visible than in Egypt where the first package tour was established by Thomas Cook in 1869. Gregory (2001) has argued that there is a 'vital continuity between cultures of travel in the past (in particular those cultures of travel established by European and North American tourists to Egypt between 1820 and 1920) and travel in the present which becomes visible as a form of 'colonial nostalgia' (2001:112). These travel experiences that were recorded in literature, photography and painting (and later through cinema) have retained such an extraordinary degree of appeal to contemporary tourists that today we find that the 'fatal attractions of colonial nostalgia are inscribed within contemporary cultures of travel' (2001: 113). Just as Said argued that Orientialism was legitimized through the constant citing of one text by the next in order to construct a 'scientific' authenticity to the discourse of colonialism, so contemporary tourism has invented traditions (Hobsbawm 1983) of colonial nostalgia that fill tourist itineraries and establish tourism as a force that claims to speak the truth about other places and cultures. The 'truths' that are created by the repetition of these nostalgic cultures of travel elevate, mobilise and privilege the subjectivity of the tourist/traveller, fixing the objectivity of the travelled upon. They also contribute to the imaginative creation of spaces of modernity and its supposed opposites and they go on to become a crucial element of the sexual 'ethnic encounters' that take place within these tourist landscapes.

In this chapter I will explore how these vacationscapes that were first created over 100 years ago continue to be informed and validated by the paths created by colonial travelling. I draw upon Gregory's (1999, 2005) analysis of Victorian travel writers in Egypt and compare this to discourses present in British adventure traveller tourism, in particular a talk given by a tour guide from the UK adventure travel company *The Imaginative Traveller* at the International Travellers World exhibition in Earls Court London in 1999.

Tourism is regularly divided into hierarchical categories, perhaps the most common being the distinction between traveller and tourist. While the tourist is often a feminised figure who travels in large groups and consumes parodic reconstructions of authentic cultural products, the masculine subjectivity of the independent traveller who travels alone 'off the beaten track' supposedly leads to a less mass-mediated 'authentic' experience.

However there is so much overlap between traveller and tourist (as we shall see package tourism even offers its own version of independent travel called adventure travel) and because so many people occupy both positions at different times in their life, I will use both terms quite loosely. All forms of tourism today – package tourism, adventure travel, independent travelling or a mixture of these forms of travel – offer different opportunities to experience an 'ethnic encounter', whether it is visiting a native village or getting to know the waiter at your hotel.

Tourism and the Colonial Legacy in Egypt

The term 'Middle' or 'Near East' used to describe the countries of the Eastern Mediterranean, Northeast Africa and Southwest Asia geographically positions the area in relation to the 'Far East'. And indeed the colonisation of Egypt by competing British and French administrations in the nineteenth and twentieth centuries was, in many ways, a by-product of earlier colonial projects in Southeast Asia. Occupying Egypt meant control over crucial trade routes that linked India and the rest of Asia with Europe, culminating in the construction and control of the Suez Canal when it finally opened in 1869.

Although several proposals for a French occupation of Egypt had been advanced in the seventeenth and eighteenth centuries, it was Napoleon's invasion that first brought Egypt under European colonial control and influence.[1] Under the control of what was seen to be a weakening Ottoman Empire, Egypt was perceived in Europe as open for exploitation. Accompanying the military and naval forces of France, and later Britain, came European merchants and dealers who established flourishing business communities in the major cities, especially Cairo and Alexandria. Joining them came hundreds of archaeologists, literary scholars, architects, artists, geographers, explorers, travel writers and scientists to investigate, dig up, map, draw, write and re-write and most importantly 'discover' the European-imagined Egypt into being (Said 1978; Gregory 1999). As Said and many others since have argued, this led to the establishment of a new discipline of Orientalism (study of the East), defined as 'a corporate institution for dealing with the Orient' by,

> …making statements about it, authorizing views of it, describing it, by teaching it, settling it, ruling over it… (1978: 3).

Although the French occupation of Egypt lasted just three years (1798–1801) it was a major turning point when the country was exposed to European military forces, systems of administration and ideologies that would have lasting influence. During the following century Egypt would become the object of competing policies between France and Britain, a part of the 'Eastern Question' and the intense focus of a new intellectual tradition in the West of Egyptology – an 'ology' that took off when a group of Bonaparte's soldiers 'discovered' the Rosetta Stone, a stone tablet with a trilingual inscription making it possible for European scholars to decipher hieroglyphs for the first time.

With an Ottoman Empire generally felt to be in decline from the outset, the European intellectual focus on Egypt concentrated on its past at the expense of its present. This past was used, much as Ancient Greece was and still is, to establish a discourse on the origins of European civilisation (Bernal 1991). Egyptology became very fashionable in Europe – made even more popular by

---

1   From the 'Encyclopedia of the Orient', www.lexicorient.com.

the accounts given and pictures painted by Victorian scholars who flocked to the region. Orientalist art and monuments were collected and brought back to an eager audience exposed to new monuments of Empire, and introduced through these collections to new themes such as cultural cross-dressing, performance and display at the international exhibitions, and contemporary museological practice (Hackforth-Jones and Roberts 2005). Egypt was also drawn into the European imagination through artist's impressions of Egypt, its cities, inhabitants, the river Nile and its Pharaonic temples. An Egypt that was portrayed as full of decaying ruins (reflecting and reinforcing the idea that Egypt's greatness was all in the past) with a population dressed in clothes that – for a European audience – resembled the costumery of the Bible. Such work had a profound impact on nineteenth century Europe and, as Europe's nearest 'Other', it is unsurprising perhaps that it was Cairo and the Nile river that became the first foreign tourist destination to be offered by Thomas Cook in 1869 (the same year that the Suez Canal opened).

For the most part travel writing during the British presence in Egypt, whether by men or women, both reflected and informed the dominant discourses of the time. As Said has argued these discourses were largely concerned with legitimising the colonial project through the establishment of an Egypt and Middle East composed of exoticising, Orientalist stereotypes of the region's history, landscape and people. Crucially writers on 'the Orient' must always locate themselves in regard to the Orient:

> ...this location includes the kind of narrative voice he adopts, the type of structure he builds, the kind of images, themes, motifs that circulate in his text – all of which adds up to deliberate ways of addressing the reader, containing the Orient and finally representing it or speaking on its behalf (1978: 48).

Theatre, Text, Scripting...and Film

Much of the groundwork in the creation of the tourist imagination lies in the practices of colonialism that often 'wrote' newly occupied places into being for the reader at home. The colonising gaze was translated and disseminated – and in so doing arguably became far more powerful – through the medium of theatre and text.

The power of the written word within the colonialist project to spread the 'gaze' of the eyewitness traveller has been noted by Said:

> ...people, places and experiences can always be described by a book, so much so that the book (or text) acquires a greater authority, and use, even than the actuality it describes (1978: 93).

For Said, the Orient was (and is) a 'theatre' for the West with the representation of places and landscapes making up the 'text'. In both imagery and text, of the place and the people, the resulting Orientalism was used by the intellectual elite of the European powers to maintain the project of colonialism, act as a counter-strategy against the fear of the unknown and in doing so help define what is Western or European by defining what it is not – Oriental. Their work, as Mitchell (1988) says, was necessary for the colonial project that needed a country to be readable, 'like a book'.

Building on Said's metaphors of theatre and text in the construction of Orientalism, Gregory (1999) argues that the consequent production of travel and tourism is a 'scripting,' that is:

> …a developing series of steps and signals, part structured and part improvised, that produces a narrativized sequence of interactions through which roles are made and remade by soliciting responses and responding to cues (1999: 115).

Gregory has chosen the term scripting in order to focus on the actual practice of travel and its performative nature. Scripting, he argues 'accentuates the production (and consumption) of spaces' and 'brings into view practices that take place on the ground' (1999: 115). Examining the scripting produced through the literary efforts of European and American travel writers visiting Egypt at the end of the nineteenth century he argues they constructed an Egypt for themselves and their readers which was a 'transparent'[2] space and,

> …exposed the gaze of the observer who had the power – and the duty – to sweep aside the mask, or in a visible sexualized project of discovery, to remove the veil (1999: 116).

Today's theatre of tourism has the added influence of cinema and television and while contemporary tourism is often portrayed as a predominantly visual activity (Urry 1990), it is not always the visual activity at the site itself but the reproduction of iconic imagery that is the most influential. The following section examines some of the enduring methods used to stage and perform 'Egypt' expressed in Gregory's accounts of Victorian travel writers that can still be found in the independent travel industry in the late 1990s. In particular I refer to a talk 'Egypt: Not Just A Pile Of Old Ruins'[3] given by tour guide Adam Greener from *The Imaginative Traveller* (a UK-based adventure travel tour company that specialises in 'adventurous' tours to the Middle East).

In the next chapter I adopt the same approach – comparing the work of Victorian women travel writers with a contemporary talk on women and travel given by two women who run an independent travel agency – to examine the ways in which

---

2   The idea of a 'transparent space' is also crucial to imaginations of the desert in Europe which will be examined in later chapters.

3   'Egypt: Not Just A Pile Of Old Ruins' was part of a series of talks offered at the *Independent Travellers' World* held at the London Arena on 5 February 1999.

Victorian women's approaches to the ways of performing and staging travel are still with us today.

Travelling through Time

Representations of people, places and landscapes in Western literature and popular media do not function alone, but are distilled through travel to the sites of colonial encounters and accounts. It is the way Western tourists travel that builds up and reinforces imaginations of tourist landscapes. As Gregory notes:

> The routes of most tourists are routinized, and each trip in its turn contributes to the layering and sedimentation of powerful imaginative geographies that shape (though they do not fully determine) the expectations and experiences of subsequent travellers (1999: 117).

The travel writers he cites visited Egypt between 1820 and 1920. Nearly 200 years after these travellers first published their accounts of Egypt, the 'routinised' routes and the sites and sights they mapped out have gone on to make up much of the itinerary of both contemporary package and adventure travel holidays – whether it is a trip to the Valley of the Kings by donkey with *Explore Worldwide*, seeing the Pyramids in Cairo with *Thomas Cook* or a relaxing luxury Nile cruise with *Bales Worldwide* affording you the opportunity to see the 'real' Egypt from the comfort of your cabin. Like their colonial predecessors scripting helps to constitute the modern tourist 'as spectator-voyeur, as consumer-collector and, above all, as sovereign subject' (1999: 146).

As mentioned previously, in mid-nineteenth century Egypt it became customary for travellers from Europe and North America to hire a large houseboat (called a *dahabeah*) with cross-sails to sail up and down the Nile River and visit the archaeological remains in and around Cairo and Upper Egypt. Reading books by previous visitors who had also sailed in these boats was often an essential part of the voyage. The boat trip was, according to Gregory looked upon as the 'defining experience of tourism in Egypt' and 'being in the same boat as their exemplary predecessors provided ordinary tourists with a precarious guarantee of the authenticity of their own experience' (1999: 119).

Travelling by boat gave the tourist traveller a suitable distance from which to observe Egypt at large and the accompanying associations with other travellers that had come before, of literally being in the same boat as them, gave the travellers a sense of security and the confidence to interpret what they saw from a sovereign perspective. The boat also provided a space which could be considered a place of modernity which could be filled with all the comforts of home, and territorially belonged to the visitor, not the visited upon. The tales of life on the *dahabeeah* mapped a 'double geography:' 'On one side, tourists had to be assured that it was possible to inspect the ancient and the exotic from the comfort and security of the modern, or at least the familiar' (1999: 119).

This positionality of being in the middle of the Nile provided a suitable distance from which to view the landscape safely and modernly – an Egypt of books written and of history dug up, validated by the traditional form of transport and the traditional ways of life of the simple Egyptian villagers that one saw from the boat.

> On the other side, tourists also had to be reassured that these incursions of modernity had not destroyed the very object of their trip: that, contrary to the anxieties of belated Orientalism, 'the Orient' was still available for their inspection more or less as they imagined it.' And the 'modern' exhibitionary process of archaeological excavation and display itself, plus the scriptings of the travel writings that proved and 'police' the sights of a (still) exotic Egypt (1999: 120).

Travel is still an uncertain activity, and the reassurance of reports given by previous visitors is no less important than that all important search for 'authenticity'. Travelling by boat along the Nile is as popular an activity for tourists and travellers visiting Egypt today as it was then, just as reading other previous visitors' experiences of Egypt in travel and guide books is. However *dahabeeahs* are no longer the main boats used, having been replaced by either the smaller 'traditional' *felucca* or a luxury cruise ship for 'tourists'.

The British tour operator *Insight Vacations*, for example, offers 'premium escorted tours and cruises for discerning travellers'. Their Egypt tour offers accommodation in a hotel 'originally built in 1886 to attract the nobility of Europe' and a luxury cruise that offers a 'visual feat' of 'scenes that have changed little for centuries'. In other words the best way to access this ancient, mystical and timeless land, is through the modern facilities offered by the tour company.

For Adam Greener's *Imaginative Traveller* a cruise boat is not authentic because it isn't 'traditional.' The *felucca* is 'the only way' to travel on the Nile:

> These are the traditional boats that they use for the Nile…it's absolutely great fun…rather than these flash cruise boats that so many people go on…you just lay out there and relax for the day, stopping off at different temples, different small villages, it's all about just watching the way that life goes along the Nile (Greener 1999).

The boats might be differently constructed in terms of their relationship to the local but the role of travelling by boat on the Nile is in many ways the same – the enabler of distance and the correct positionality – an appropriate viewpoint for the sovereign subject of an ancient unchanged Egypt either authenticated by a traditional form of transport or made comfortable safe and luxuriously modern.

> What I really like is when we actually leave the towns such as Aswan and start
> getting scenery...it's just wonderful to see village life which has not changed for
> thousands and thousands of years and we're not disturbing (sic) as we go along
> in the feluccas, nice and quiet. Here is a shot of the women who are carrying sort
> of water jugs on their head, as you can see they've been getting water, probably
> from the local oasis[4] (Greener 1999).

Greener's sleepy Egypt 'has not changed for thousands and thousands of years'.
He is also very optimistic that by viewing this ancient Egypt from a safe distance
his 'travellers' will not be disturbing it or ruining its fixed timeless nature with
incursions into their modernity. By ensuring its fixity in time he is, as Gregory
says of the early twentieth century writers, viewing Egypt as anachronistic space
'in which past and present existed outside the space of the modern.' In this way
travel writers, says Gregory, 'claimed to open an imaginative (and extraordinarily
presumptuous) passage into an ancient land' (1999: 121).

In the geographical imagination of both the present day tourist, and Victorian
travel writer, Egypt is an antithesis to modernity, and these imaginations – achieved
through reading the work of travel writers, and observing 'traditional life' from a
distance, enable European visitors to feel as if they have left modernity.

The strength of these tourist geographical imaginations can be seen in their
persistence, and ability to survive events such as the 1939–45 Second World War,
Egyptian independence in 1952, the Suez crisis in 1956 and the many modernist
engineering projects of nation-building such as the Aswan High Dam constructed
between 1960 and 1970. Other areas of the formerly colonised world have their
own geographical imaginations that are no less powerful. Wilson (1994) argues that
tourist imagination of paradise is so strong in Hawaii that the islands are effectively
prevented from developing economically, lest they ruin their picturesque, tribal/
native lifestyles and the resulting income from tourism. But if we know *how* the
tourist and its industry create a place lost in time and space, the question remains
as to *why* such an outcome is deemed so desirable.

According to Gregory the construction of Orientalism is not a 'distorted
mirror' as Said suggests. It is 'real' in the sense that it is real for the spectators.
Here we can see how the production of such an Egypt, then as now, also has real
consequences such as the construction of an Egypt described by Greener above.

When Greener was asked why Egypt is presented to his travellers as being part
of the past, not part of modern life, he replied that he was merely being responsive
to the needs and desires of his clients who do not travel to find similarities, but
difference:

> We give people what they want and they want to go out and see interesting
> areas which are often the more rural areas, and they're often slightly less

---

4   Here Greener might be mistaken as it is unlikely there is an oasis so near the Nile.
The women are probably getting water from the Nile or one of its tributaries or canals.

developed...in the end it's supply and demand...For me, being honest with you, the modern parts of these countries are very interesting but I do go out there to try and lose myself in the other parts, things that are not similar to this country where I live, to me the adventure of travel is to go somewhere where it is very, very different and that other side exists, but if I did a slide show full of shots of towns and cities and told everyone they're all on the internet and this, that and the other, whether people would be as interested I don't know (Greener 1999).

Greener's motive for travelling in Egypt and maintaining such a geographical imagination of a lack of modernity, of a place that represents 'that other side' is to 'lose himself'. This desire – to escape both from modernity and from oneself – is a recurring theme of tourism and women's sexual tourism in particular that I will discuss in more detail in later chapters.

By describing the modern traveller's desire – achieved through travel to the Third World – to enter the past and leave the modern, as the mere seeking of difference, Greener is portraying this type of tourism as innocuous and essentially harmless. By presenting this imaginary as the result of a simple desire for a break from the norm, the reductionist and stereotypical nature of the resulting binaried 'difference' remains unchallenged:

At the end when we talk about tourism and that's why we're here, and in the end we're all tourists, we often go for the reason that we want to see something different from our culture, we want to see someone living in a different way (Greener 1999).

The seeking of difference partially explains why parts of Egypt that do not fit in with this image are so carefully ignored but it does not explain why difference is so carefully constructed around the past, the traditional and the very 'unmodern'.

One difference between the travellers of the late nineteenth century and early twentieth century and those of the late twentieth and early twenty-first century is that the tourist gaze today relies more on images, moments and events created by the 'modern' technologies of film and television, especially those that consist of reworkings of the texts that came before them.

Today few brochures and guidebooks fail to mention Agatha Christie's 1937 murder mystery *Death on the Nile* although it is usually the 1978 feature film (dir. John Guillermin) that is referred to. Its enduring appeal can be seen by its adaptation for the stage by Christie in 1944, its debut on American television in 1950, a feature film version in 1978, a BBC Radio Four version in 1997 and a popular television version in 2004 (It also became a computer game in 2007 and was published as a graphic novel by HarperCollins in 2007).

The following, for example, is an excerpt from the website of Canadian tour company *IDTravel Inc*:

Aswan is a must during your visit to Upper Egypt... You will not be disappointed by the many historical sites including the Unfinished Obelisk, the Temple of Philae, Egypt's finest temple at Abu Simbel and the world famous High Dam. Spend time relaxing in the setting of Agatha Christie's 'Death on the Nile,' take a stroll through the botanical gardens on Kitchener Island, or hunt down the many bargains in the local market (www.idtravel.ca/factfile.html).

The tour operator *Insight Vacations* introduction to their Egypt itinerary adopts a similar tone:

Welcome to Egypt – a mystical and timeless land, where ancient and modern live side by side. On arrival in Cairo, you join a long list of travellers, from the ancient Greeks to Agatha Christie, who have been seduced by Egypt's archaeological wealth. You are met at the airport and transferred to your elegant and sophisticated Cairo hotel (http://www.insightvacations.com/world/index. php?tour_code=N945W).

Here the 'ancient and modern' still live side by side – Egypt remains an anachronistic space where the modern presumably refers more to the comforts and facilities offered to the travellers rather than the sights themselves. Other colonial imaginaries (especially those that have been transposed into major cinematic epics) can be found in many other activities offered to Western visitors to the country especially those that involve transportation.

While travelling 'as the locals do' for tourists/travellers in the late nineteenth century was often the only option available to them, the modern adventure traveller is just as adamant about 'authentic' modes of transport, many of which only continue to exist as available forms of transport because of tourist demand.[5] Greener however does not justify this preference as a desire to experience how 'locals' or Victorian travellers *used* to travel, but as they still travel today:

When I go in places like Egypt, yes, I do use camels to go out in places in the desert. Another way to go is by donkey and again it's how the locals travel. It's just great fun going by donkey, a lot of these donkeys have a mind of their own... you just sit there and hope for the best (Greener 1999).

This is another method, like the *felucca* trip down the Nile, by which the people are kept in the 'past' in the eyes of the tourists. Farmers in remote villages in Egypt do still use donkeys and some Bedouin might still travel by camel. But in general

---

5   The most obvious example of this is the horse-drawn carriages in Luxor, but it is also true to some extent for *feluccas* on the Nile, donkeys in the Valley of the Kings, horses at the Pyramids at Giza and camels in the Sinai. Although horses, camels and donkeys are still used by Egyptians and Bedouins, their tourist use is far higher.

they prefer Toyota pickups and the vast majority of camels and donkeys in Egypt are there to provide for tourist demand for these modes of travel.

While heritage tourism is a global phenomenon, it is marketed very differently in Europe and North America. Tourists visiting London, for example, can 'experience' Victorian London by taking a ride on a renovated Charabanc. However it is never suggested (or imagined) that Londoners still use this mode of transport today. Tourist imaginations like Greener's help to fix countries like Egypt in the Western geographical imagination as belonging to a different time, and in so doing, as Fabian (1983) argues, denies them 'coevalness'.

Greener and much tourist literature on Egypt suggests that visitors can go back thousands of years, however in fact companies such as his are offering a return to a specific moment in *Western* history. Firstly there is the generalised ancient time – or even timelessness of Pharaonic Egypt – of Antiquity. But this time is mediated through the imagined experiences of colonial explorers. Other histories, both ancient and modern, are erased. Egypt's history of powerful Islamic dynasties or recent post-independence history barely gets a mention. Instead Greener's imageries go back to the most major Western experience of Egypt – that of colonialism, when the Orient was written, painted – and later filmed –into being.

A ride on a camel often inspires conversations and imaginaries of the Irish actor Peter O' Toole playing the English officer T.E. Lawrence in *Lawrence of Arabia* (dir. David Lean 1962). This film – and others such as the Oscar winning film version of Michael Ondaatje's 1993 novel *The English Patient* (dir. Anthony Minghella 1996) – highlights the British military presence of the region and its contribution to the modern tourist's geographical imagination. A sense of the colonial history of Egypt might also come from a more personal source, such as a relative having been stationed in Cairo or elsewhere in the Middle East as a soldier during one of the wars in the last century.

The Ethnic Encounter

While agency is seen to lie mostly in the actions and experiences of the tourist, not the toured upon, Gregory suggests the colonial scripting of Egypt depended on – and can therefore be influenced by – the actions of local people.

> But these touring productions also have multiple authors in quite another sense, because they depend upon – and can be interrupted, dislocated and reworked by – the practices of local people who are involved in them (1999: 117).

Gregory differentiates between Victorian travel writers and adventurers who he feels merely reiterated the dominant colonial discourse of the time and those who perhaps enabled some local 'disruption' by immersing themselves in Arab culture through activities such as adopting the local dress and learning the language.

Using a combination of Lefebvre's 'production of space' and Latour's (and others) actor-network theory, Gregory describes how the construction of the space of Egypt was not a straightforward project enacted solely by the most powerful European agencies (such as banks, archaeology and tour operators). It was also brought into being by 'the knowledges, skills and labours of countless local merchants, interpreters-guides, boat owners, sailors and donkey boys' (2001: 115).

These heterogeneous networks mapped an Egypt, according to Gregory, where some discourses and practices became privileged while others became marginalized. In this way 'modern' and the 'traditional' commingle in such a way 'that the partitions between these spaces and the privileges accorded to them are constantly interrupted, confounded and dislocated' (2001: 116).

The agency given to local people and their ability to disrupt the colonial (and tourist) gaze is a theme that runs through much work on Victorian and Edwardian travel writers. Mills' (1991) analysis on women travel writers of the same period, which will be discussed more fully in the next chapter, also refers to several authors of the period whose sympathy with other cultures was proven by their desire to experience ethnic encounters – to interact with local people and 'do as the locals do'. Yet this division between writers who got to know their subjects and those that merely observed is problematic. As Mills herself notes, such a reading is often partial, as authors often exhibit an ambivalence that veers from sympathy to patronising comment. Using Sir Richard Burton's account of his journey to Mecca and William Edward Lane's travels in Egypt as examples, Mills points out the popularity of the travel writing technique of placing the narrator as a Westerner in disguise who is able to outwit the natives into accepting him or her as a 'local' and is therefore able to 'penetrate' their society, particularly travelling to places usually out of bounds to foreigners.

> The westerner in disguise is a figure of great textual power since it demonstrates
> great knowledge to a western audience, and at the same time it asserts even
> greater power over the people of the colonised country since they are represented
> as being fooled by the disguise (1991: 140).

In a similar vein the disguise of the fluent Arabic of Swiss explorer Johann Burckhardt is credited with his 'discovery' of the ancient Nabatean city of Petra in Jordan in 1812. The 'adventurer' Henri De Montfried, often mentioned in travel guide books such as *The Rough Guide: Egypt*, adopted the practices and customs of the local Bedouin population of the Red Sea coast and the Sinai desert in Egypt to the extent of becoming involved in their hashish smuggling. Many women also saw opportunities in dressing up as a local, an 'ethnomasquerade' (Sieg 1996, Konuk 2004) that was not only cross-cultural and racial, but also cross-gendered (which will be discussed in the following chapter). In the next section I will examine some of the colonial influences of the expectations and meanings placed upon tourist and traveller ethnic encounters.

The Guide

Tour companies such as *Thomas Cook, The Imaginative Traveller, Explore Worldwide* and even *Dragoman* directly and indirectly reference the colonial past (even through their names). They also employ 'local' guides to act as interlocuters, essential and reliable guides that are so necessary to Westerners when they traverse another cultural space.

The local guide (and/or driver) often turns out to be one of the most influential people any traveller or tourist is likely to meet while on holiday. The guide is the primary ethnic encounter in many cases and they also serve as gatekeepers who might go on to coordinate and instigate further local encounters. With such a potentially powerful position (despite their lack of privilege in other ways) it is hardly surprising that their trustworthiness (or otherwise) is a repeated motif of both colonial and modern day tourism. The guide acts as a pivotal intermediary between the 'other' and the Western visitor; they help the visitor understand, and negotiate on the visitor's behalf to help them attain what they seek. Greener stresses how his tour company use guides that will enhance the experience of visiting Egypt – *Salam* is helpful, trustworthy, and reliable – he is a friendly native – a guaranteed authentic ethnic encounter that allow the visitors to do things 'that locals do':

> It's an incredible experience being with someone like Salam and travelling around Egypt, not only for the fact of course that he speaks Arabic and he can translate but for the fact that he is so friendly and so good to be with and everywhere we go he can tell us so much about the history and culture of this wonderful country (Greener 1999).

The 'friendly' construction is so much part of the host-guest relationship of tourism and the tourist narrative that in many cases it is something of a given. As I will discuss later it is also very much part of the construction of locals as sexually available in sex tourism destinations.

Gregory notes how Victorian travellers were encouraged in guide books of the time to secure 'the services of a reliable dragoman, a local interpreter-guide,' (1999: 120) yet they were also warned of the dangers of embarking on such a venture. Potential guides might well present themselves to travellers but they were warned to treat them with suspicion and given instructions on how to deal with them and other natives they might come into contact with, such as the boat crew. The love/hate relationship of fear, loathing and desire of the 'other' was often most concentrated in the relationships that ensued between the guide and the guided.

> Largely ignorant of language and even custom, most tourists were more or less completely dependent on their dragoman; but this reliance produced an unease, even a distrust that could spill over into outright contempt...The dragoman was assumed to act purely in his own interest, and his local knowledge was typically

marginalized by attributing it to guile, malice or simple ignorance against which the tourist had to prevail (1999: 23).

The potential distrust and fear of the 'local' remains in the discourse that surrounds the modern traveller, shown when Greener attempts to allay potential fears his audience might have about the use of a guide, by stressing his qualifications, his reliability, his ability to interpret and understand Western values and his friendliness.

> Salam is an Egyptologist and he's qualified. Now to be a guide in Egypt you have to be a qualified Egyptologist, you have to have gone to university. He's got an incredible knowledge of places...he's also a bit of a card...we use him a lot because he's very reliable, he speaks excellent English...he can read hieroglyphics off tombs and tell me stories like it says this and this says that (Greener 1999).

While the tourist might aim to maintain a position of 'sovereign subject', they also occupy a far weaker and more vulnerable position – of strangers in a strange place who do not speak the language and do not know how to navigate and understand what they see. The guide is therefore a potentially powerful (and also threatening) figure. However, Greener later warns – if they go by themselves and use an 'unqualified' guide – their behaviour and skills cannot be guaranteed. It's a risky business.

Doing as the Locals do

While several travel writers such as Edward Lane adopted local identities (dressing as locals, learning Arabic and taking an Arabic name) in the name of research for his book, it is not surprising perhaps, that however attractive the idea of dressing 'as a local' was, it was also considered a dangerous proposition, which might symbolise the first step towards the loss of one's own civilisation, a traversing of the boundary between 'East' and 'West' so ably created by colonial discourse. It was therefore important to establish rules and Martineau (1848) was one of many writers who stipulated exactly what the European woman in Egypt should wear.[6] Victorian travellers had strict dress codes – but the very act of going abroad led to the development of a whole new sartorial genre – travel clothes for the Empire. While these new fashions still met many of the exacting standards for modesty required by Victorian society, they did tend to be more loosely fitting and less formal than clothes worn at home – arguably opening up an intermediary space for experimentation with identity. While the prevailing fashion for caps and frills was considered impractical, broad straw hats and goggles to protect against the sun

---

6   H. Martineau (1848), *Eastern Life, Present and Past.*

were stipulated. Local headware such as the *tarboosh* (more commonly known now as a *fez*) used for the same purpose as a broad straw hat, was only thought appropriate if worn in private.

Gregory suggests that, at first travellers were more open to the idea of adopting local dress codes, but by 1870, when formal tours were introduced by Thomas Cook, this practice was all but gone. Murray's *Handbook* published in 1873 listed what is now seen as the classic Victorian travel uniform: tweed suits, a felt hat with white muslin or a pith helmet. Again, adopting the clothes of the locals was frowned upon and the popular 'red *tarboosh*' was condemned as 'no respectable European resident in the country would think of appearing in it in public.'

For Gregory this is just one more example of how 'lines were drawn and attempts made to police the inevitable interactions across them.' (1999: 127) But the clothing of English Victorian travellers and Egyptians was also crucial to geographical imaginations of place and crucial props in the theatre, text and scripting of the Orient.

Differences in dress between locals and Europeans during the colonial period was crucial to the ascription of different identities and differential relations to modernity as Gregory shows with an excerpt from A. Edwards *A Thousand Miles Up the Nile* (1877).

> Here are Syrian dragomans in baggy trousers and braided jackets; barefooted Egyptian fellaheen in ragged blue shirts and felt skull-caps; Greeks in absurdly stiff white tunics, like walking penwipers...Swarthy Bedouins in flowing garments; ...Englishmen in palm-leaf hats and knickerbockers, dangling their long legs across almost invisible donkeys; native women of the poorer class, in black veils that leave only the eyes uncovered...dervishes in patchwork coats.

Western visitors today still expect to see locals decked out in traditional (not modern) and colourful costumes. Greener's talk was accompanied by a slide show depicting 'traditionally' dressed Egyptians; men in *galabeyas* and women in *hegab* (veiled).

Ethnic encounters are the primary selling point for adventure travel holidays, but these encounters are still based upon the assumption of a significant cultural difference and a sufficient lack of modernity. Nearly all brochures that sell holidays to Egypt (and other formerly colonised countries) emphasise this cultural difference through images of 'native' figures, especially women and children in passive poses in 'traditional' dress. In its 1999 newsletter, the British company *Explore Worldwide* emphasises that the most important experience to be gained by holidaying in Egypt comes from interacting with the 'natives' whose 'friendliness' is innate:

> But perhaps the strongest impression is made by the Egyptians themselves – busy shopkeepers, village children, Nubian felucca sailors and the desert Bedouin are

alike in their welcoming hospitality and respect of visitors (*Explore Worldwide* January 1999 Newsletter).

With adventure travel the emphasis is not just on looking – the tourist gaze – but also on 'interacting' with the local culture through people (the body) albeit in a highly pre-scripted way.

> As I said, the most important thing about travelling in any of these places, really, it's just the people…these are just going to be a few more shots of people I've met along the way… (Greener 1999).

Bhabha (1994) has argued that Western preferences for a binary 'them' and 'us' approach to the world has led to a desire to dominate or colonise 'them'. Maintaining and creating these binaried differences of the 'other' are often achieved through images of the body.

Objectification of 'natives' is crucial to their construction as living representatives of un-modernity, or pre-modernity. The images are not just about a difference in culture but a spatial and temporal difference. Egyptians are *felucca* sailors (a traditional form of ship now only maintained because of the tourist demand), desert Bedouin, village children and busy shopkeepers – all romantic, exoticised images of a people and country based on the first experiences of colonial travellers. They are 'traditional' Egyptians, engaged in 'traditional' pastimes.

Egyptians in 'modern' dress are nowhere to be seen in Greener's Egypt, only those who, through their appearance, embody the experience of an ancient and colonial Egypt are shown.

Doing as the locals do not only involves travelling on a local form of transport (like a donkey), it also involves dressing as a 'local' taking part in a local activity. The most popular activity that is part of nearly all Nile Cruises is a *Galabeya* party where people don local costume and attempt to perform a traditional and cultural 'belly-dance'.

> Well the kind of things that people do is to go out and buy a belly dancing costume like this…and if you want to do some belly dancing, well next thing you know you put your belly dancing suit on and away you go…when in Egypt, when anywhere in the Middle East, go and see a belly dancer, you should do, it's all part and parcel of the local culture. The local men often go out to watch belly dancers… (Greener (1999).

Although the folk dance *Raqs Sharqi* is part of the Egyptian culture, belly dancing is a derivative colonial version that developed after it was performed at the Chicago World Trade Fair in 1893 (Lorius 1997). The sensuality of its movement and its implicit sexual content was very popular with the conservative Victorian population and it soon became a popular past-time in Egypt to go and see 'belly dancing' in the nightclubs that sprung up to meet this new demand (1997: 37).

The exotic and sexual appeal of the Orient although rarely explicitly mentioned in tourist brochures is never far away. A sighting of an Egyptian or Bedouin man in a *galabeya* might well remind the tourist of Rudolph Valentino in the 1926 silent film, *Son of the Sheik* (sic) which created an enduring fantasy of an irresistible desert dwelling Arabian sheikh decked out in transgendered apparel, holding captive an attractive, partially clothed dancing girl with a transparent veil. Images that stemmed in part from the populist Victorian Orientalist reinterpretations of Richard Burton's and Edward William Lane's (1840) translations of *A Thousand and One Nights* The sheikh and his son, both played by Rudolph Valentino, portray the Arab man as handsome, passionate, and seductive. It isn't necessary to have actually seen these films, they have become part of our contemporary Western cultural approach to the Orient through short clips re-shown on TV, the continued use of Orientalist imagery in other films, advertisements and TV programmes and magazine fashion spreads.

'Dressing up' as a local (often involving some kind of idea of cross-gendered dressing) – if done in the safety of a tour group on a boat in the Nile – offers more opportunities to engage safely with the 'other' and yet remain in control of the experience. Sieg (1996) has defined an ethnomasquerade as 'the theatrical embodiment of other ethnicities by a subject that thereby exercises power and simultaneously hides it', while Konuk refers to it as 'the performance of an ethnic identity through the mimicking of clothes, gestures, appearance, language, cultural codes, or other components of identity formation' (2004: 1). Konuk goes on to connect this to Bhabha's idea of mimicry, which he argues is one of the most effective forms of colonial power and knowledge making – where an identity is constructed that is 'almost, but not quite' as the original:

> Colonial mimicry is the desire for a reconstituted, recognizable Other and constructed around the ambivalence created by the potential eradication of difference between the original and the copy (Bhaba 1994: 85).

In a clear example of tour companies reproducing their own version of colonial tradition for tourist consumption, Greener explains the cultural transvestism of the *Galabeya* party. The addition of the social lubricant of alcohol and dancing provocatively in revealing clothes of the 'other' hints of the racial sexual fantasies involved in this performance of the Orient.

> As well as that there's buying Galabeyas. The kind of thing that we would do is probably all go out and buy some of the local clothes. There's often a Galabeya party on board which is great fun, everyone dresses up in the local clothes, has a bit of a party and tries a bit of belly dancing. It's good fun to do that kind of thing.

> (The slide changes to a view of the boat deck)

Ten o'clock in the morning after a Galabeya party. There you go, no one on deck because everyone's got hangovers. So there you are, on the Nile, on Amy (the name of the boat) ...(Greener 1999).

Conclusion

Tourism, especially the tourism that involves ethnic encounters is, if anything, more focused on the consumption of the 'other' than colonialism which was preoccupied with so many other targets. This consumption focuses on easily identifiable markers of difference of time and place such as traditional dress, homes and customs, that are seen to constitute authenticity for the consumer. Of course this journey to the 'other' is also a commercial transaction, so fraught with the potential for the tourist to be mis-sold the product. Perhaps more pertinently the tourist is nearly always aware of how their presence simultaneously creates and invalidates the authenticity – making it too 'touristy' – even if this threat is caused by other tourists rather than their own subjectivity.

With so many ethnic encounters constructed around nostalgia for colonial encounters and representations of authenticity, existing stereotypes of the toured held by the tourist are hard to break down. In the Middle East the stereotype of the un-modern and traditional Egyptian farmer or Bedouin tribesman is often meant positively, even offered to counter another stereotype of Arabs as 'shifty and deceiving' or 'violent fundamentalist terrorists'. But one stereotype is just being replaced by another and perceived differences – that people in the traditional, un-modern south are warm and friendly compared to the colder northern people of modernity – are still being highlighted. Focussing on their friendliness and 'respect' for the 'visitor' does little to challenge the notion of tourist as 'sovereign subject' and is also arguably a part of their sexual construction as willing and compliant in response to the needs of their visitors, which I will discuss further in the following chapters.

Gregory concedes, as Frow (1991) has argued, that all tourism might be irredeemably nostalgic. He explains how his use of the term 'colonial nostalgia' departs from Rosaldo's 'imperialist nostalgia' (1993) used to refer to the yearning for what colonialism itself has transformed. Instead he argues that the guidebook and the tourist brochure are examples of a colonial nostalgia that re-inscribe and fuse two moments:

The first is a nostalgia for colonialism itself, a desire to re-create and recover the world of late Victorian and Edwardian colonialism as a culture of extraordinary confidence and conspicuous opulence....The second moment is more oblique. It involves the recovery not only of *fin-de-siècle* claims to power but also its claims to knowledge. For these guidebooks and brochures imply that we are not 'too late' – that we can steal a march on the anguish of 'belated Orientalism' – and that we can do so, ironically enough, by imaginatively transporting ourselves back to its definitive period...We might now revisit that past, go behind the elaborate stage-machinery and finally, realise that we have been the architects of the illusion all along (2001: 140–1).

Although Gregory suggests that 'routinised routes' can be disrupted and reworked by interaction with local people, and local-tourist encounters can dislocate, interrupt and confound the spaces between modern and traditional, he also argues that Victorian and Edwardian travel writers constructed an Egypt 'with little or no reference to those who lived there' (1999: 145). A contemporary tourist-local interaction based upon such nostalgia for Victorian and Edwardian ways of seeing and doing, however still allows for and often reinforces the construction of the host population as the 'other', as objects rather than subjects. For it is difference that is kept paramount, rather than any similarity.

Gregory suggests the reason why the colonial past remains so appealing to contemporary tourism and surprisingly resistant to change, is due to the nostalgia generated by the '*seductiveness* of colonial power' (2001: 112). The imaginative geography of the adventure traveller is constructed through a far greater degree of reference to those who live there, through the ethnic encounter – but they too look back to this Golden Age of travel. There is little evidence that their geographical imaginations are any closer to how Egyptians might see themselves – or like others to see them – than Gregory's travel writers. For Gregory the agenda behind the myth making then was the British occupation of Egypt. Today the imaginative geographies of tour company, guidebook and traveller continue to produce an Egypt that attempts, at least, to fulfil Western desires to be in a place without modernity, to observe traditional life from a distance for Egypt to be a 'transparent space' of the Orient. Relationships with the other remain simultaneously desired and feared. Activities like belly-dancing, dressing as locals and employing a guide might be full of the (sexual) promise that constitutes geographical imaginations of the Orient, but they can also cause tension and conflict with their potential to call the tourists' sovereignty into question.

These imagined destinations create expectations among visitors that the actual country, cruise, hotel etc, cannot always manage to fulfil. Based on a romantic interpretation of a nostalgic colonial past, the reality of a holiday in Egypt can also lead to tension and conflict. There are also opportunities for visitors to reassess their expectations and Orientalist influences. According to Liechty (1996) while a locality is a social construction – a place transformed from space by social relations that generate shared experiences, the tourist resort is a 'translocality' – a 'hot spot' populated by tourists and locals that carry heavy imaginary burdens because the tourist's geographical imagination is 'increasingly mass-mediated and 'liberated' from the confines of the locale' (1996: 99). In a reverse of Rosaldo's 'border zones' (places where the Third World implodes on the First) Liechty's tourist spaces are translocalities – 'zones in which the First World implodes into the Third' (1996: 99).

Said's conception of Orientalism has been criticised by Garcia Ramon and Albet-Mas for being a 'homogenous discourse expressed by a unified colonial subject upon a unified colonised object, both of which are male' (1998: 229). Women and gender differences in general are also (mostly) absent from Gregory's construction of scripting and geographical imaginations. In the next chapter I will explore these arguments within a gendered context, by looking specifically at the work of female Victorian and Edwardian travel writers and comparing their work to the writings and commentaries of contemporary female travellers and writers.

Chapter 2
Writing Women's Travel

The link between the literary output of Victorian and Edwardian travel writers and the sustainability of colonialism has been made often enough (Said 1978, Gregory 1999, 2001, Lewis 1995); a link that emphasises the power of the written word to make authoritative statements and disseminate the desired information to a far wider audience than that of the 'eyewitnesses' to another landscape and culture. Furthermore the nostalgia for this kind of travel writing and production of knowledge about other cultures is so powerful that contemporary guidebooks and tourist brochures (Gregory 2001, Beezer 1993) still rely heavily on their romantic vacationscapes, augmented by a new media – cinema – that has been eager to create lush, exotic versions of these stories, such as *Lawrence of Arabia* (dir. David Lean 1967). As we have seen in the previous chapter, the ethnic encounter is a crucial component of contemporary tourism to the Middle East, particularly among adventure travel tour companies and backpacker tourism. Yet this ethnic encounter is constructed around Orientalist imaginations and only locals that are seen to represent some kind of antithesis to Western modernity are sought out. Tour operators and guidebooks continue to offer a holiday/travel experience based on Victorian and Edwardian colonial geographical imaginations of landscape, place *and* people.

The ethnic encounter is also offered as a way out of Orientalist production of knowledge. According to Gregory, colonial Egypt was produced as 'a space of constructed visibility' a space that could be 'rationalized' with landscapes that were panoramically 'timeless', 'authentic' and 'real'.' (2001: 115) Yet through actor-networks the assignment of power (privileged – rational or marginal – customary) to the construction of Egypt as 'modern' and/or 'traditional' is constantly being 'interrupted, confounded and dislocated.' (2001: 116) Gregory's scripting of Egypt is also never presented as a completely closed circuit where local people are passive participants of an Orientalist theatre. There always remains the possibility to disrupt, confound and/or re-work scripting through 'interaction' with the locals.

Said has been criticised by feminist theorists for presenting Orientalism as a predominantly male experience for both the coloniser and colonised (Lewis 1995, Garcia Ramon and Albert-Mas et al. 1998, Yegenoglu 1998) and Gregory's notions of colonial nostalgia, scripting and geographical imaginations have also tended to pass over the issue of gender.

This is surprising because women writers on the Orient are noted for their focus on ethnic encounters and their ambivalent relationship to the colonial project. If any group of people might be said to have been capable of repositioning the voice of the local, of attempting to 'disrupt' or 'confound' the dominance of Orientalism, it would be these Victorian and Edwardian women who travelled to the Orient.

Although travelling was then (and arguably still is) seen as a male pursuit, Victorian and Edwardian women who could afford it also travelled (most often in Ottoman Egypt and the 'Levant' but also elsewhere in Africa and Asia) and many published accounts of their journeys upon their return. While there was a period during which they were largely forgotten, interest in their work has grown in the last few decades with the development of the feminist movement and the rise in Western women's travel in general. In Britain at least, much of the credit for the revival of interest in Victorian and Edwardian women travellers goes to the feminist publisher Virago Press who in 1983, reprinted the books written by Isabella Bird, Mary Kingsley, Gertrude Bell, Emily Eden, Lucie Duff Gordon, and Lady Mary Wortley Montagu in the *Virago Travellers Series,* and hailed them as feminist 'pioneers'.[1]

In the late 1980s and early 1990s their feminist credentials were explored further by writers and journalists, such as Russell (1988), Birkett (1989) and Melman (1991), and through popular TV series such as the 1999 Channel 4 production of *Maiden Voyages*. At the same time their relationship to the colonial project and Orientialism (in particular their preference for the ethnic encounter) began to be examined in more detail in the academy by Blunt (1994), Phillips (1999), McEwan (2000), Mills (1991), McClintock (1992), Pratt (1992) and others.

Today the ethnic encounter is still more associated with women's travel than men's. By looking at the work of Victorian and Edwardian travel writers explored by the authors above, and comparing their work to the writings and commentaries of women who are travelling – and writing about their travels – today, this chapter will explore how the re-enactment of the journeys of these late nineteenth and early twentieth century 'pioneers' have gone on to shape contemporary ethnosexual (Nagel 2003) tourist-local encounters and how they are a crucial part of the global trend towards postcolonial (nostalgic) travel in the early twenty-first century.

Women and Travel Writing

Although the first woman who published her travels to the Orient, Lady Mary Wortley Montague, did so in 1718, most women travelled and published much later, during the relatively short phase of 'high imperialism' at the end of the nineteenth and early twentieth centuries. A period when, Mills notes:

> ...a new colonial relationship emerged, where formal conquest, annexation and administration became the most common relation between Britain and certain other countries, and Britain declared herself to be an imperial nation (1991: 2).

---

1   See http://www.virago.co.uk/about_virago.asp?TAG=&CID=&PGE=&LANG=EN

It was also a period when it became easier for women to travel, partly because during the consolidating phase of colonialism settlement of women was encouraged as a means to combat the feared miscegenation that might occur among communities of predominantly male settlers.

However, even if Victorian and Edwardian women were more free to travel, they were still very much confined to a path that had been laid by men and it was always clear they were travelling in a male milieu – within a masculine subjectivity. As Clifford argues, travel was something men did.

> 'Lady' travelers (bourgeois, white) are unusual, marked as special in the dominant discourses, practices. Although recent research is showing that they were more common than formerly recognized, women travelers were forced to conform, masquerade, or rebel discreetly within a set of normatively male definitions and experiences (1997: 31–2).

Mills and others (Birkett 1989, McClintock 1992, Pratt 1992, McEwan 2000) argue that Victorian and Edwardian women's travel literature has been the focus of a discovery of sorts because it was 'hidden' or ignored for many years. In addition women's writing was also qualitatively different from their male counterparts because of their ambivalent relationship to the project of colonialism.

According to Mills, women as travellers were informed by different discursive frameworks and pressures. As women living in patriarchal societies they could not adopt the imperial voice with the same ease as men. They were also hampered by prevailing notions of femininity that did not allow for women's travel, especially the potential to experience physical hardship and the possibility of being alone among (male) strangers.

In addition, unlike their male counterparts, women rarely travelled on 'official' voyages of exploration, their travels were not usually accompanied with letters of formal introduction and they were not expected to carry out some grand project.[2] One of the oft commented upon outcomes of this marginal position in the colonial project was that, as travel writers, they concentrated on describing people rather than places. Their work was on behalf of the Empire but, as Mills points out, their gender meant they were unable to adopt a straight-forwardly imperial voice and they exhibited an 'ambivalence in their position in relation to power' (1991: 20). This ambivalence, says McEwan, meant that women didn't 'quest' and didn't chart 'uncharted territory' and weren't as imperial in their imaginations.

In contrast, men, according to Mills, were more likely to describe people as a sum total of body parts, highlighting their difference from the European 'norm' rather than giving them full 'individual status.'

In this way, by concentrating on culture and people, these women – who had already transgressed boundaries of mobility associated with Western femininity

---

2   One notable exception to this was Gertrude Bell who did all three.

– would be confining themselves to more acceptable subjects of discussion for their gender at that time; people rather than politics.

Women travel writers were therefore more likely to align themselves with the colonised subjects than their male counterparts because they both shared a marginal positionality in relation to the colonial project and were just as susceptible to being treated as inferior. Mills, for example, suggests that because these women were 'othered' by Western masculinity, they were capable of a level of reflexivity that was noticeably absent from the work of male writers:

> ...women writers, as well as being concerned with interaction with others, were, because of their socialisation as sexualised objects of a male gaze, generally more aware of the way the narrator appears to others, of themselves as objects (1991: 98).

But even Mills concedes that this was by no means a trait in all women writers and there were many women who did not identify with the 'natives' on any level. And even those that expressed sympathy for them, interspersed such commentary with the dominant colonial theme of condescension towards the colonised. For example, Mills points out that Mary Kingsley, one of the most famous female travellers in Africa who wrote extensively about the 'natives',

> ... for all her supposed affiliation with the cannibal Fans, still thought that they were inferior and like children, a standard colonial statement (1998: 92).[3]

Nevertheless, because women travellers were positioned differently to male travellers they are generally seen to occupy a double position, so that while they were in alignment with an imperial discourse they were also affiliated to the colonised. For Mills this means their work, 'constitutes both a challenge to male Orientalism and a different form of knowledge about other countries (1991: 99).

While it is important to acknowledge how the output from female travel writers differed qualitatively from their male counterparts on many levels, it is also important to acknowledge that this difference did not always constitute a 'challenge' to male Orientalism, but in many ways complemented it. If male travel writers were limited in their production of knowledge about the local population, then perhaps women writers could be said to have filled this gap. As McEwan says:

> Women travellers may not have 'discovered', mapped and explored 'new' territories, but they did add to the imagery constructed about the empire. Moreover they influenced how this imagery was mapped onto the imaginations of the majority of people in Britain who did not have first-hand experience of (such) areas of the world... (2000: 215).

---

3   Kingsley (1897/1965).

McEwan highlights the potential problems in the construction of women's travel writing as ambivalent. Said may have only spoken about an Orientalism articulated by and about men, but that doesn't mean there weren't other, perhaps ostensibly more marginal, Orientalisms in circulation, that still exerted a powerful influence on the colonial project.

Contemporary Women's Travel

Victorian and Edwardian women travel writers, such as Gertrude Bell, Mary Kingsley and others have become such an important influence that stories of their lives and their work can dominate contemporary women's geographical imaginations of the places they have visited and written about. In an interview for *The Guardian* newspaper with Angela Neustatter, Viv Taylor-Gee, the producer of the 1999 UK Channel 4 documentary series *Maiden Voyages*, argues that although these women were travelling in colonised countries, they were not colonisers because they concentrated on the personal and while 'men want to conquer things, women often want to conquer themselves.' The series explored the lives of these travel pioneers, and explicitly linked them to contemporary British women adventure explorers who claim to have been inspired by their Victorian and Edwardian predecessors. Another *Guardian* article about the series shows a 1902 photograph of Lady Constance Mackenzie, a 19-year-old girl who was one of the wealthiest people in Britain at the time. She is sitting on a donkey that is being led by a native man. The message is clear – 'pioneer' women of the late nineteenth century and early twentieth centuries were early feminists who have inspired contemporary women's travel as a search for liberation:

> ...women who have cracked fears and taboos, who have dared to go for personal development or simply set out boldly in the footsteps of their Victorian and Edwardian forebears, often express the experience as Laura Marshall (one of the women featured in the TV programme) did: 'It made me realise that being a woman doesn't have to limit me in the ways I had felt before' (Neustatter 1999).

The Ethnomasquerade and Honorary Man

The adoption of a local identity by dressing up as a native while travelling has been mentioned in the previous chapter. Certainly men who indulged in this form of travel (such as Richard Burton, Henri de Montfried, T.E Lawrence and William Burckhardt) have received a lot of attention from Said and others (such as Garber 1992, Silverman 1992), while men who vacation in this way today have also been examined by Boone (2003). For women perhaps the advantages of such a travel strategy were even greater. While dressing as a native woman (which included veiling) in order to be able to freely move and mingle with the locals was initially popular among some Victorian and Edwardian women when they travelled in the lands of the Empire, later visitors, perhaps emboldened, sometimes went further by adopting a male identity to increase their freedom of movement. If travel as a woman transgresses the gendered boundaries of movement, dressing as a man is an ambiguous activity. For while it ostensibly bows to the accepted norms that confer extra travelling privileges onto men, it also had the potential at least to allow Victorian and Edwardian women travel writers to travel in other directions, perhaps even to explore gender divisions.

Stevenson (1982) suggests that women travel writers in the colonial period adopted the personae of men mostly in order to gain freedom. For a writer like Mary Kingsley, simply being away from her own society allowed her to escape the gender-based restrictions of that society and this allowed Kingsley to pursue her own imagination by 'becoming a man' (1982: 15). As a feminist pioneer Kingsley is supposed to have challenged accepted notions of gender, but it could also be argued that such a strategy was a pragmatic compromise that implicitly acknowledged women could only access certain areas of personal freedom (including sexual freedom) if they became 'men'. As Mills points out, this implied 'that the only type of free woman that there can be is one who imitates a man, thus concurring with the view that the male is the norm' (1991: 92).

This quest for personal freedom shown by so many Victorian and Edwardian women travel writers certainly reveals a degree of ambivalence towards a standard viewing of Orientalism. However, much of the identity changing that went on among female travellers was not from Western woman to Western man, or even Western woman to native woman, but Western woman to *native man*. Garber (1992) suggests that 'Westerners have looked East for role models and for deliberate cultural masquerade – for living metaphors that define, articulate, or underscore the contradictions and fantasies with which they live' (1992: 352). One example was the writer Isabelle Eberhardt, who often travelled as a Bedouin man in North Africa. Again, as part of their trope as feminist pioneers, Edwardian and Victorian women ethnomasqueraders have been presented as engaged in a subversive activity (Garber 1992, Silverman 1992). Garber for example argues that when this form of cross-cultural, cross-gendered dressing is carried out by women travellers from Europe and North America, there was some kind of subversiveness attached because they disrupted the binary of male and female.

However, as McClintock has replied, 'Cross-dressing can...be mobilized for a variety of political purposes, not all of them subversive. That...cross-dressing disrupts stable social identities does not guarantee the subversion of gender, race, or class power' (1995: 67).

While there were practical reasons cited such as ease of travelling and supposed access to a greater degree of authenticity in effect these women were engaging in a short term strategy of embodiment of the other, rather that an overt identification with local men (Konuk 2004). As noted in Chapter 1, dressing as a local was often, rather than a disruption of the Orientalist project, if anything, presented as proof of the Victorian and Edwardian traveller's superiority; the colonial subject could become the 'colonised' or at least pass for one, but never the other way round – the colonised could never assume the identity of the colonial.

As Konuk (2004) also points out the ethnomasquerade was very similar to Bhabha's notion of mimicry within the colonial project. This form of ethnomasquerade after all, assumed that people were constituted as locals through their costume and manners alone and just by mimicking this local costume (for example a *galabeya*) and learning an Arabic dialect, they could pass for a local. It also seems very much related to the desire to experience some form of 'authenticity' while travelling, as this form of dressing supposedly gave the traveller some kind of cloak of invisibility. This invisibility solved the problem all tourers experience of potentially ruining the authenticity of the object of their gaze by their presence, and could therefore offer the costume wearer leading to a greater degree of 'reality'.

Which local identity they chose to mimic is also significant. We have already seen how adventure travellers in tour groups are encouraged to dress sexily as belly-dancers as an excuse for an exoticised party. Just as with Western men travellers going native, women dressing as locals – especially dressing as men – speaks more of travel as theatre and performance and travel allowing experimentation with gender identities; an argument we will return to in the following chapters.[4]

Although, as we shall also return to in the following chapters, the practice of dressing as a local woman is still very popular among women travellers, it would seem the adoption of a local male identity is a colonial-era activity that has not been carried into contemporary tourist practice by women travelling today. North American and Western European women no longer have to adopt a male personae to occupy a position of privilege in male space, they can do so as women. Most travel, especially in Arab countries like Egypt rely on the use of public transport such as the train, the taxi and buses. It can also involve a lot of hanging around in public spaces, the cafes, train stations and bus stations, that are – again particularly in Egypt – male spaces. Spaces local women tend to use only when travelling with other members of their family. Other tourist spaces, such as souvenir shops, hotel lobbies, museums, – again, particularly in Arab countries like Egypt – are also predominantly male spaces. Therefore it is common enough in modern travel, just as it was for the likes of nineteenth century female travellers like Gertrude Bell, for Western women to feel they have adopted the identity of an honorary man when they traverse these spaces.

As honorary men who occupy a position of privilege in male dominated public space, Western women are understandably more likely to meet and socialise with men than women. This often means that the ethnic encounter is a gendered

---

4   In later chapters I discuss the plot of Egyptian novelist Ahdaf Soueif's *Map of Love* (2000) a Booker-nominated novel set in late nineteenth-century Egypt that features an upper class British heroine who becomes an Egyptian woman, then a male French aristocrat and finally a Bedouin tribesman by a quick change of costume all in the space of a few hours in order to facilitate her journey of seduction (by an Egyptian man) from Cairo to the Sinai.

encounter that first takes place in male public space. While this can lead to a sexual encounter as we shall see, it also results in women identifying more with local men than women. In a *New Statesman and Society* review of their collection of stories from contemporary women travellers, Davies and Jansz (1999) noted how many women travellers they had contact with, not only identified with men, but also experienced a widening gulf between them and the women in the country they were visiting:

> Many of the travellers who wrote to us expressed an uneasy guilt about identifying more closely with men, whose greater access to education and contact with the outside world provided a more immediate common ground (1998).

The masculinising effect of First-World status on being a woman when travelling also besets researchers in the field. The Israeli anthropologist Smadar Lavie lived among the Mzeina Bedouin of South Sinai whilst recording their lives, and related with pleasure how her gender allowed her to socialise with Bedouin women, while her status as a Westerner also gave her the privileges of a man and enabled her to mix freely with the Bedouin men.[5]

The position of women who travel from imaginations of modernity to the tourist spaces of supposed un-modernity in the 'Third World' changes as a result of this journey, offering many benefits to Western women to explore new freedoms and gain new privileges. But this freedom gives the ethnic encounter a peculiarly one-sided slant. Like the mimicry of the other the freedom goes only in one direction, it is not reversible and cannot be said to automatically lead to any sense of 'solidarity' with local men or women (even if you dress like them). Resulting encounters might be gendered, even sexualised, but offers no evidence that any Orientalist stereotype or production of knowledge is being disrupted through actor networks. This new identity accorded to First-World women who travel is often constructed around the status of honorary man; the new freedoms are masculine freedoms that originate from the possession of a greater economic and social wealth than those that are being visited. Travelling as an honorary man must therefore challenge the notion of modern women's travel as a guilt-free personal goal development activity first pioneered by Victorian and Edwardian ladies, an argument which will be discussed in more detail later.

Women's Travel and the Re-production of Knowledge

Representations of places and people in travel brochures, newspaper and magazine articles and guidebooks certainly help the process where patterns of travel and

---

5   Lavie claimed that this ambiguous man–woman status enabled her to be treated as both a man by men and a woman by women – yet at the same time she remained somehow sexless when she carried out her fieldwork among the Sinai Bedouin.

travel activities get passed on and replicated through time. Travel articles in particular are often targeted specifically at women and generally fall into two main (overlapping) categories: what to pack and issues of safety.

Travel guides for women, such as *Hints to Lady Travellers at Home and Abroad* by Lilias Campbell Davidson (1889), began to appear towards to the end of the nineteenth century in response to the small but growing numbers of women travellers to the colonies. As Mills points out, their presence revealed one of the many contradictions in the prevailing notion of femininity. Full of advice on how to travel without compromising the prevailing norms of female respectability, they still encouraged women to transgress those norms by travelling in the first place.

Most of *Hints to Lady Travellers at Home and Abroad* is taken up with warning Victorian and Edwardian women of the many dangers – mostly sexual – facing white women abroad. However, the remainder consists of recommendations of what to take along in order to maintain the same degree of comfort that was enjoyed at home plus a list of medical supplies to pack for accidents.

Over 100 years later and women travellers are still being advised about the very same issues. At the 1999 *Independent Traveller's World* held in the London Arena the packed seminar on 'Women and Travel', organised by independent travel agent Polly Davis and travel writer Maggie Moss covers just two main areas: packing advice and how to avoid (mostly sexual) danger.

What Women Pack

The luggage of the traveller is not just a selection of their belongings, it also includes items which people only use when, and for, travelling; items which it is assumed cannot be obtained in the country of destination.

In 1889, Davidson suggests women should take a small flask of brandy, plasters, scissors, smelling salts, a bath, needles and a cushion, suitably covered with chintz or satin, for putting under the feet.

In 1999, Polly Davis, the owner of Bristol-based travel agency *Marco Polo*, also gives a detailed list of what to take which includes a sleeping sheet, mosquito net, moneybelt, torch (on a string), army knife (on a string), scissors, sewing kit, water bottle, lighter, candle, mirror, padlock, pegless washing line and string. Her clothing list includes one set of warm clothes, a respectable set of clothes for immigration control and customs, walking shoes, sandals, warm jumper/fleece, thermal underwear, cotton trousers, waterproof and hat. Next is the medical kit which should contain mosquito repellent, malaria pills, sun cream, water sterilisation/iodine tablets, antihistamine tablets, antiseptic cream, aspirin, plasters, bandages, cotton wool, sterile needles, oral rehydration sachets, antibiotics and contraceptives.[6]

---

6   Davis (1999) 'Women and Travel' at the *Independent Traveller's World*, London Arena.

The message that you are leaving civilisation and modernity behind when you leave your home to 'travel' appears to be clear. Everything is to be bought before departure, because, although this equipment is necessary in order to be able to traverse wilderness safely, it is assumed that these items will not be available in the wilderness. The technologies of modernity are necessary for travel in spaces that lack modernity, they are necessary for travel in general, but it is also implied that these technologies and the products they create are only available in the First World. I asked Davis why these goods could not be bought upon arrival at the destination; a young woman from the audience replied that it would not be possible because you would be 'in the desert or jungle.' Yet most of these products are produced in the very same countries adventure travellers are travelling to and are easily available there. Travelling destinations as places of modernity and spaces that are crucial parts of a globalised economy, would seem to interfere with the popular notion of Third-World travel in the West, that it is *from* a place of modernity, *to* a place of precivilisation, a place of nature, not cities (unless ancient and derelict) or modernity and that travel itself is a movement from a place of mobility to a place of fixity. How women's tourist geographical imaginations of place deny as far as they can, the impact of contemporary global economic forces and move the space of the Westerner in very interesting ways, while attempting to fix the space of the travelled upon, will be discussed further in the following chapters.

(Sexual) Danger

Avoiding danger for women travellers today generally falls into two subsets: firstly the general events that are covered by travel insurance policies such as getting ill, having something stolen or being in an accident, and secondly the more gender specific (but not always) danger for women of sexual harassment and rape. Maggie Moss, herself a co-author of the *Handbook for Women Travellers* (1987) presented the major part of the seminar, 'Staying Safe' (1999). The audience of (mostly) young white British women were advised how to behave abroad in order to be safe; advice such as stick to busy areas, dress conservatively, don't go out alone late at night and so on. While this could be said to be appropriate advice to all single Western women when they are out in public places in their own societies, here it is being stressed, not only because men in other societies are seen as more sexually threatening but also because women who travel in pursuit of personal freedom often (deliberately) suspend their normal awareness of appropriate and inappropriate dress and behaviour. Western women who travel leave behind many of the 'safety' behaviours that are the norm in their own country (Mårdh, Arvidson and Hellberg 1997). The act of travel is often seen as a means of removing many societal restrictions and travel to the Third World in particular evokes feelings of being 'out of time and place'. First world travellers often find themselves in a new (masculine) space that they cannot read with accuracy, but one that is also very connected to the privileges often accorded to Western women travellers while travelling in Third-World countries. Being a stranger, and the process of 'othering', can mean they are unaware of the social norms in the country they are visiting, but more often than not women just assume that these social norms do not apply to them because they are not 'locals' (unless of course they attempt the ethnomasquerade). This can place some Western women in an interesting but no doubt dangerous position – when they travel they do not feel they have to adhere strictly to the norms of female behaviour in the society they are visiting, but as I will show in later chapters, they also often do not maintain their *own* gender mores because they are away from home.

One example of this is perhaps travellers' dress codes. Often when travellers leave their country they start to (un)dress very differently to how they dress at home, wearing less and less. They also create a space through travelling where this behaviour is considered 'normal', especially by following routes and staying in tourist spaces populated with Western tourists and travellers who behave and dress in a similar fashion. They are therefore often blindly unaware of the spatial boundaries that affect the dress codes of 'locals', which leads to their transgression of spatial boundaries of social behaviour and dress, such as continuing to wear bikinis when away from the beach in nearby shopping areas, restaurants and even when crossing the road. A sense of the tourist and traveller as 'sovereign subject' and a feeling of territorial ownership over the tourist spaces they inhabit is partly responsible for this common behaviour, but so too is a desire to break with the social customs and gender restrictions of the societies they are coming from, something that will be discussed in Chapter 5.

It is not only travel seminars designed for young women in Europe that focus on the dangers of women travelling, particularly those that choose to do so alone. It is almost impossible to find an article or programme in the popular media that does not reiterate this idea and offer the female traveller advice. This is especially noticeable when the countries to be visited countries, are viewed as masculine such as Egypt. The notion of travel as a metaphor for personal freedom is inseparable from its other interpretation – that of sexual freedom and therefore, where women are concerned at least – sexual danger. These simultaneously held binaries are redolent of the fear of, and desire for the exotic in Western discourse that will be discussed further in Chapter 4. Women who take these attitudes on board and travel in places like Egypt often express surprise when they discover how safe they actually feel, yet this fear remains a defining experience of travel for Western women.

Travel is often also considered dangerous for your sexual health, especially if you are a woman. For while being a woman confers privileges upon the traveller, it also implies sexual danger. Similarly the advantages of being white and Western contain both advantages and vulnerability. Unless your audience is lesbian, a guidebook for women will not discuss the possible pleasures of sex and romance when travelling but the dangers are always written large. Guides for both Victorian and Edwardian women travellers and their contemporaries highlight the vulnerability of a woman travelling, and warn against the sexual threat from 'native' men when they travel, especially when alone, yet at the same time they also stress the special attention (or protection) their gender affords them.

Davidson, for example, warns her readers about the dangers – including sexual dangers – of travel, yet she also adds:

> Much has been said about the danger to women, especially young women, travelling alone...As a rule women travelling alone receive far more consideration and kindness from men of all classes (Davidson 1889: 63 cited in Mills 1991:101).

Today's travel media rarely mentions women's travel without referring to the underlying sexual threat. A 1999 article for the travel section of *The Observer* by the guidebook author Moss, is typical of the genre exemplified by the title 'You want to be a woman alone, but are you safe?' Yet, after spelling out all the reasons why women should be worried, Moss, like her Victorian counterpart, tries to mitigate these dangers by referring to the advantages women have over men when travelling.

> Despite the potential pitfalls, women travellers often find themselves on the receiving end of great kindness and hospitality (Moss 1999).

Women are also, she says, more likely to have greater sympathy and empathy with the 'natives', being more open, aware and sensitive, and more interested in the people than the scenery, unlike men. Women are also 'more flexible'.

Travel as a means to obtain personal freedom is often inseparable from sexual freedom (and sexual danger). The erotic possibilities of travel were also very much a feature of Victorian and Edwardian travel, perhaps just as much as they are today. As Littlewood (2001) notes, by the end of the nineteenth century women tourists travelling to southern Europe (a favourite destination for 'love', especially Italy) outnumbered those of men (2001: 62).

The connections between travel and sex, although often expressed quite openly in literature concerning (heterosexual and homosexual) men's travel (such as Paul Gauguin in Tahiti, Andre Gide in North Africa and others), were not usually made explicit in literature on women's travel where metaphors of 'personal freedom' were more likely to be used. Instead they focused on the sensuality of the climate, landscape and people, as in this letter from Gertrude Bell telling her family about her 'Desert Excursions' in the desert surrounding Jerusalem.

> The Sheikh and all the swells came to call and took me into the village to look round. Dear, nice people! I am sorry to leave them. I haven't left them yet, however, for the Sheikh, Ibrahim, is still in my tent door as I write. He makes well, I must say, being singularly beautiful. It is a hot, hot night (Bell 1939: 103).

Women alone, especially when travelling, are very much caught up in a paradoxical binary of fear and desire, forever associated with sexual availability *and* vulnerability, sickness *and* health. 'Casual travel sex' as one medical journal calls it, when practised by women, is defined as a high-risk activity that can lead to the infecting the rest of the population with disease, especially AIDS.[7] But if travelling (especially to hot, tropical climates) is considered sexually dangerous for your health, it is also a 'cure' for other ills. Travel to the warm south was prescribed as a cure for Victorian and Edwardian women's invalidity and a beach holiday is still considered a great restorative for stressed overworked women today. Despite growing concerns about skin cancer and the ageing affects of sun exposure, a few weeks in the sun are still seen as a health boost and health resort/spa tourism is booming. It is often the same destinations recommended for containing health-giving properties that are also the most popular destinations for women's sexual travel.

Conclusion

Re-enactment of Victorian travel aside, contradictions and tensions continue to constitute the discourse surrounding women and travel, particularly when the travel is to developing countries and involves ethnic encounters. By adopting a supposedly male pursuit, in being mobile and then by acquiring some of the privileges of a masculine persona while travelling, women can gain greater freedoms when they travel. By exercising their femininity they supposedly can access even more advantages though the (protective masculine) tendency of their hosts to look after them. Theoretically at least, women can have the best of both First and Third Worlds, and of both genders.

Yet acceptance of these freedoms seems to stop at sexual freedom. Dominant discourse in the West determines women are at greater risk when travelling; the message remains that travel (for heterosexual women) involves sexual risk rather than greater sexual opportunity. Women who have sexual encounters with 'natives' while on holiday continue to pose a threat to hegemonic notions of femaleness in the West.

Traveller accounts have been mentioned by Said (1978), Gregory (1999) and Lewis (1995, 2003) and others, as one of the most successful means of transmitting the production of knowledge about the Orient. These accounts tapped into a powerful and attractive emotional geographical imagination of the Orient, so much so, that contemporary tourism, hungry for nostalgic journeys to the past, often attempts to re-produce these imaginations, and travellers and tourists

---

7 Their research concluded that women who already indulged in 'high risk' activities such as smoking cigarettes and drinking were more likely to have 'casual travel sex' whilst abroad and it was therefore necessary to target this 'high risk' group of women to prevent the spread of AIDS and other STDs.

are encouraged by tour companies and the popular media to re-trace Victorian/ Edwardian footsteps or even re-enact their adventures.

However it is also important to note that the Orientalist knowledge produced in the work of the Victorian and Edwardian traveller was by no means uniform and, in particular, attitudes have been found to differ quite radically according to the gender of the author. It has been suggested (Mills 1991, Pratt 1992, Blunt 1994, McEwan 2000) that women's ambivalent relationship towards the colonial project and their lack of power compared to their male counterparts produced a different approach to their subject particularly regarding their accounts of encounters with local people.

As we have seen, the production of knowledge by Orientalism was very much predicated on othering, a process of representation of non-Western people that Bhabha (1994), Hall (1997) and others argue is most powerfully exerted through binaries. As Hall notes,

> They seem to be represented through sharply opposed, polarized, binary extremes – good/bad, civilized/primitive, ugly/excessively attractive, repelling – because different/compelling because strange and exotic. And they are often required to be both things at the same time (1997: 229).

For Bhabha (1994) the stereotypical 'other' in colonial discourse is primarily defined through differences of race and sex – in other words, through the body. This places the body in two economies – the economy of pleasure/desire and the economy of 'discourse, domination and power'. 'Otherness' is at once an object of desire and derision and an articulation of difference contained within the fantasy of origin and identity (1994: 66).

Perhaps a good example of how the binary of racial and sexual difference operates across time and space in a colonial context can be found in the marriages of Impressionist painter Paul Gauguin (1848–1903) to a Danish woman and – at the same time – to a 13-year-old Tahitian girl. As Pollock (1994) notes, Gauguin was so sure these two worlds could exist for him on a separate plane, he sent a portrait of his young Tahitian bride to his Danish wife.

> Two wives, two systems, two places, two female figures in the painting whose viewing apex is one man – the apex of a triangle between two wives, two systems, two places... These two women mark a geographical and cultural distance, traversed by the masculine European – the point for ethnographic transactions between cultures and genders (1994: 65).

Here the tropical journey is reproduced as a sexual quest and the other – the native – is in this case, a woman. The other is defined and structured through oppositions – here/there, home/abroad, light/dark, safety/danger and so on.

In the European imaginary, the white woman is mother, sister, wife opposed to the negative mirror-image of the black woman, the dark lady of the sonnets, savage, sexual and eternally other...It is her irreducible strangeness which gives her value and makes her an object of white man's fascination...but she is never recognised as a subject in her own right (1994: 66).

Pollock acknowledges that privileged Victorian and Edwardian women also participated in this journey to 'otherness', but she concludes that their gender was subsumed by dominant discourses surrounding race and class. Women travellers therefore, tended to adopt a similar perspective as their Western male counterparts when it came to attitudes to non-Western women. Difference of race and culture took precedence over a shared gender because 'colonialism colours gender, and gender inferiority can be displaced by cultural power expressed through race' (1994: 82).

Whether Victorian and Edwardian or present day, guidebooks and travel literature are still guides to travel, and don't necessarily reflect the reality of women's travel. They stress the ethnic encounter but tend to shy away from direct mention of that most intimate of ethnic encounters – the sexual encounter – unless to focus on the threat it poses to women travellers, particularly those who travel alone. Yet as more and more First World women travel, the sexual ethnic encounter is often something they travel for, rather than fear. In the next chapters I will explore these contradictions by looking at the sexual encounters that take place between European women on holiday in the Sinai and local men.

Chapter 3

Paradise and Deserts – Tourist Landscapes on the Margins of Modernity

Introduction

As Europe's nearest 'other', tourism to places in the Arab world cannot help but be influenced by Orientalism and in Chapters 1 and 2, I explored how this region has preoccupied European sensibilities for centuries, perhaps mostly notably by it being designated other through its geographical location and referred to as the East or Orient, a foil for the West and its identity.

We have seen how contemporary Western tourism has been shaped by the journeys mapped out by Victorian and Edwardian travellers and how hotels, brochures, guide books and tour companies rely on a colonial nostalgia for this selective history to sell destinations like Egypt. This nostalgia relies upon and reinforces a view of countries like Egypt as 'anachronistic space' (McClintock 1995: 30), and employs 'the concept of fixity' in the ideological construction of otherness' (Bhabha 1994).

McClintock's argument that colonised space is presented as the site of 'prehistory' and the conquering nation is the location of the Enlightenment, stretches through to our everyday relationship with modernity and its supposed opposites in the 'Third' world. Tourist space today in formerly colonised countries is a space where you can visit a colonial version of prehistory. In tourist resorts like Sharm El Sheikh, Nuweiba and Dahab these anachronistic spaces are simultaneously reduced to sites/sights on tourist itineraries and expanded to offer the postcolonial modern tourist a new space of colonialism to visit them through.

As we have also seen Orientalism was a process of representation, often carried out by Victorian and Edwardian travel writers who provided their readership with exotic accounts of the places they visited. Today it is not necessary to have read the original work because their output has been reproduced and reinterpreted in our media throughout the twentieth and early twenty-first century. Indeed, today places become holiday destinations simply because they were used as locations for the cinematic versions of these stories. Petra in Jordan gained widespread publicity when it was used in *Indiana Jones and the Last Crusade* (dir. Steven Spielberg 1989) while Karnak in Luxor and the Nile cruise – are locations and activities popularised in the movie version of Agatha Christie's *Death on the Nile* (dir. John Guillermin 1978). Romantic tourist imaginations of desert landscapes, as I argued in Chapter 1, are also circulated through their association with films, though they can have a more generic appeal so that *Lawrence of Arabia* (dir. David Lean 1962) and *The English Patient* (dir. Anthony Minghella 1996) can be influential in selling holidays in the Sinai, even though they are not set there and the Sinai was not used as a location for filming. Travel brochures, shown in the excerpt below from a seven-day itinerary to Egypt and Jordan offered by the American agency *Travel In Style,* often refer to these filmic imageries as a major selling-point, offering a way-in to experiencing a place that might otherwise just appear to be a pile of rocks.

> Petra was known in the bible as Sela, and rediscovered only in 1812. You'll feel like Indiana Jones in Raiders of the Lost Ark as you penetrate into the city through a narrow sandstone gorge … (*Travel In Style*: http://www.travelinstyle. com/multi/Egypt_Jordan_Indian_Jones.htm).

Many other locations in the region are sold on the basis of allowing the tourist an opportunity to 'retrace the steps' of an influential adventurer such as T.E. Lawrence or perhaps to stay in the same hotel as T.E. Lawrence (the Baron in Aleppo, Syria) or the Cataract Hotel in Aswan – where Agatha Christie wrote her crime mystery *Death on the Nile*. Again, this influence can be indirect and can move from one desert to the more tourist-friendly Sinai or Jordan. Most tours do not actually take their groups to the exact same desert locations where T.E. Lawrence rode his camel or horse, but to the sites where his film persona 'Lawrence of Arabia' did. And while Antoine de Saint-Exupéry's work focused on the Sahara (he disappeared after flying over the Sahara desert on reconnaissance for America in 1943) the title of one of his books is used for the name of Sinai safari tour company *Wind, Sand and Stars*.

This type of travelling is based on layers of experiences of the Orient and the desert inspired by a colonial imagination and instils in the traveller a sense of going back in time that can lead to associating a country and its population with an historical, colonial past rather than a contemporary modernity. This stereotyping of place and people serves to give tourists certain expectations even before they have arrived. The Orient of the Middle East and North Africa (MENA) region has to be exotic, romantic, masculine and most of all, different.

Of course the focus of this book is the postcolonial encounter and while I will discuss how the people of the region are 'othered' in the following chapter, in this chapter I want to focus on this construction of an othered landscape and explore how these encounters can be understood in the context of the modern subject and its relationship with place considered to be outside of modernity. I will examine the imaginative and emotional construction of the two primary Sinai landscapes and argue that these landscapes are constructed in this way as part of modernity's nostalgic search for 'home'.

In order to do this I will initially introduce the peninsula and its tourist resorts. I will then explore the ways in which geographical and historical imaginations of the desert and paradise (as situated outside of Western modernity) as well as identities based on the modern subject, influence the development and marketing of this region – and the women who decide to go on holiday there. In this way, I aim to show how these women's ethnosexual encounters with local men are bound up in these temporal/spatial geographical imaginations (Gregory 1994) of place that involve an 'emotional geography' (Bondi, Davidson and Smith 2005) so that the sex/love object is not just the man but also a landscape (not always a beach) that is imagined as existing 'out of time and place' (Wagner 1977: 38).

Imagining the Sinai

Despite being one of the oldest inhabited regions of the world with claims to be the original site of written language and of many memorable Biblical episodes, the Sinai that tourists visit today is a fairly recent construction. The desert is part of the Afro-Asiatic rift valley and extends over approximately 61,000 km² from the Mediterranean in the north, to the Red Sea in the south. Since the Arab-Israeli wars in the second half of the twentieth century, the region has taken on an important geopolitical role as a 'buffer zone' between Israel and Egypt and an international peacekeeping force (Multinational Force and Observers) continue to maintain bases there.

Prior to the development of tourism in the late 1980s, the majority of inhabitants were Bedouin, mostly descended from tribes who migrated from pre-oil Arabia in the eighteenth and nineteenth centuries. There are several different tribes that can be roughly divided into three groups – the *El Tiyah*, the *Tarrabin* and the *El Touara* tribes.

The *El Tiyah* or 'lost' tribes live in the central heights north of the El Tih plateau as far as the eastern Negev or Naqab desert in Israel. Until the opening of the Suez Canal, their main income, apart from their sheep and camels, was derived from guiding pilgrims on their way to Mecca.

The *Tarrabin*, who originate from Egypt, occupy different pockets including Wadi Sudr and the north coast of the Gulf of Aqaba as far south as Nuweiba. The *Mzeina*[1] are the largest of the *El Touara* or 'mountain' tribes of the southern region who first migrated from Arabia just over 400 years ago. Today they live in settlements in El Tur about 90km north of Sharm El Sheikh on the Gulf of Suez coast, Dahab and as far north as Nuweiba. Although the southernmost region, where the resort of Sharm El Sheikh has been developed, lacks fresh water so has not been a traditional area of settlement for Bedouins, many have migrated there for work reasons, in particular the Mzeina but also other tribes (Glaser 1978).

There are two main regions in the Sinai; the flatter, more fertile plains to the north of the central El Tih plateau, and the more arid mountains and wadis to the

---

1   There are many other Bedouin tribes living in the Sinai, such as the *Alekat* who live in the areas around Serabit El Khadem in the interior, and the *Jebeliya* who live mostly around St Catherine's Monastery. The *Mzeina* and the *Tarrabin* however are the largest tribes, who because they live on the coast as well as in the mountains, have come into contact with the Egyptian government and the tourist industry to a larger degree.

south of the plateau – referred to as South Sinai by Egypt – approximately one third of the total area.[2]

South Sinai is the Sinai that is photographed, written about, and visited by Western tourists; in particular the coral-rich south-east coast of the peninsula that first became a leisure destination during Israel's occupation from 1967–82.[3] During this period, while the Sinai's military role as a buffer zone was paramount and many minefields were laid, there were also settlements of Israeli collective farms – called *moshavs,* in Nuweiba, Dahab and Sharm El Sheikh (then called Ophira), which led to certain forms of tourism aided by the establishment of a basic infrastructure such as tarmac roads and petrol stations. Many visitors in the 1970s were young kibbutz volunteers and Israelis (especially soldiers on leave) who stayed in makeshift camps provided by the Bedouin (and Israelis) in the border settlement of Taba and around the palm-tree fringed Bedouin fishing villages of Dahab and Nuweiba. The monastery and much of the Gulf of Aqaba coast were designated as nature reserves where only very basic camping was encouraged[4] augmented by three hotels, two in Sharm El Sheikh and one in Taba, 4km south of the Israeli town of Eilat.

The signing of the 1979 Camp David Accords between Israel and Egypt that resulted in the Sinai being handed back to Egypt in 1982 did not greatly affect the numbers of tourists of who came to the Sinai until 1987 when the five year hiatus on development, agreed between Israel and Egypt, came to an end.

By the early 1990s however, the tourist landscape was radically changed by projects instigated by the newly-established Sinai Governorate and Egypt's Tourist Development Authority. Although Bedouins have been the main inhabitants of the Sinai desert for over 200 years, the creation of tourist zoning effectively cut them out of the resulting economic boom along the coast. Most of this boom was focused on the scuba-diving potential of Sharm El Sheikh; it already had an airport, was much flatter which aided development and was

---

2   The north of Sinai has a very different history, local population, climate, sea and landscape and is virtually devoid of foreign tourists. What local tourism there was has declined with the political situation in Gaza. The region has more farmed land and local industry than the south.

3   Direct access between the north Sinai and this south-eastern region is limited by the lack of roads, except for those used by Bedouins. Tourist traffic and movement of people in general in the Sinai is concentrated along the coast roads and the two roads that cross the interior linking St Catherine's monastery to the Taba-Sharm El Sheikh coast road and Suez with Taba and Nuweiba on the east coast.

4   This period in Sinai's recent history is often talked about with great nostalgia by Bedouins and tourists from that period alike who suggest that if Israel still occupied the Sinai it would have remained a natural place with no development. However, with Eilat as a nearby model of what could have happened if Israel had succeeded in maintaining sovereignty, it is more likely that development was kept to a minimum by the Israeli state because it was known they would have to return Sinai sooner or later so it did not make sense to invest huge amounts of money in the area except to extract minerals.

closer to Cairo. However by the late 1980s and early 1990s Dahab had become a big draw for young Egyptian men from the Nile Valley who came to set up small businesses there and mix freely with Western tourists and backpackers. Many travellers also set up businesses, particularly diving centres, and the place soon became such a firm fixture of the backpacker circuit that many people started to move to the Bedouin beach huts on the quieter beaches of Nuweiba, near a port used for trade and pilgrimages to Mecca for many hundreds of years. Here, despite some resort development, the pace of life has remained much slower, aided perhaps by its distance from Cairo, the paucity of coral reef to attract divers and the political deadlock with Israel that has led to a failure of the *Red Sea Riviera* project that optimistically aimed to link Taba (to the north) with Eilat in Israel and Aquaba in Jordan.

In general, the Egyptian state does not encourage or promote the type of Bedouin-inspired budget tourism that Dahab and Nuweiba offer. Dusty tracks have been tarmacked and concrete walls built to block out the views of Bedouin homes from these roads. Hotel development has been encouraged to replace the more basic huts and campgrounds offered by Bedouin entrepreneurs while the beachfront has been pedestrianised and decorated with Victorian-style streetlamps. Larger hotels have built more upmarket resorts nearby and pressure upon smaller players in the tourist market to upgrade their facilities or sell up is strong. Although Dahab has flourished to a certain extent, in recent years much of the income-generating businesses have been taken over by economic migrants from elsewhere in Egypt and global big business keen to capitalise on Dahab's popularity with backpackers and divers. Recent drought conditions have also made the Bedouin's more traditional income-generating occupations of goat and sheep herding in the desert interior increasingly difficult.

In contrast Sharm El Sheikh is a bustling tourist resort with very little Bedouin influence or origin. It is also the furthest tourist settlement in the Sinai from Israel (nearly 300km), and the closest to Cairo. With no natural source of water, Sharm El Sheikh was never a Bedouin village but began life as a military base built by Israel to watch over the strategic straits of Tiran in the late 1960s. A low level salt plain with much room for expansion it has warmer winters than Dahab or Nuweiba and a far more extensive coral reef coastline in addition to the reefs in the Tiran Straits and Ras Mohamed National Park 35km up the road towards Cairo.

Initially Egyptian entrepreneurs arriving in Sharm El Sheikh added small hotels, diving centres and camps to the two hotels left by Israel. However this was soon followed by foreign investment and much larger scale tourist development projects, encouraged by government tax breaks, cheap loans and a World Tourism Organisation (and other global organisations like the World Bank) policy of the time that pushed tourism development in countries like Egypt as a primary means for general development. During the late 1980s and early 1990s the main tourists in Sharm El Sheikh were scuba divers from Northern Europe. While numbers suddenly dropped after the 1991 Gulf War, new global trends towards beach holidays found an easy ally in Sharm El Sheikh, particularly with its proximity to Europe and Russia and its winter sun appeal.[5] Although Israeli tourists continued to visit Sinai, particularly Dahab and Nuweiba, after it reverted to Egypt, in recent years their numbers have dwindled.[6]

Many Bedouins moved to Sharm El Sheikh to find work, as it became more developed, but they and the local Bedouins who live in nearby in Wadi Mandar and the fishing village of Nabq have long been viewed with suspicion by the Egyptian government. The 2005 and 2006 bomb attacks in Sharm El Sheikh and Dahab led to many Bedouins becoming targets in the Egyptian state's interpretation of the Western 'War on Terror'. Hundreds were imprisoned and a new 'security wall' (said to have been inspired by the much larger wall that separates Israel from parts of the West Bank in Palestine, now separates Sharm El Sheikh from these surrounding Bedouin settlements.

In geopolitical terms the Middle East and North Africa region (MENA) is considered to be a volatile area and events like the September 11th attacks, and armed conflict ongoing in Afghanistan and Iraq, might lead many to assume that resorts like Sharm El Sheikh are prone to a high degree of fluctuation in visitor numbers caused by this uncertainty. However, as Steiner (2009) points out, in general tourism growth in the MENA region continues to grow at a remarkable rate. This rate of growth however is not uniform, for while the more traditional heritage tourism sites such as Luxor, Petra have suffered from some decreases, the 'ultramodern' resorts like Sharm El Sheikh and Dubai (at least until the recession of 2009) have continued to grow, perhaps as Steiner suggests precisely because they lack the 'spatial, historical, and social embeddedness' that would lead to them being imagined as Islamic (2009: 2).

Indeed, apart from some minor blips, numbers of visitors arriving at Sharm El Sheikh airport have grown at great speed. Today, while diving remains popular and the laid-back, mostly Bedouin and European-run camps of Dahab and Nuweiba still attract the international budget traveller, the Sinai is primarily visited as a hotel-beach destination reached by charter flight to Sharm El Sheikh airport. Numbers of visitors trebled from 400,000 in 1996, to just under 1.5 million tourists in 2002. Another six years later and in 2008, Sharm El Sheikh airport had expanded its capacity to receive 7.5 million passengers a year. It is currently undergoing a second major expansion project to double this capacity to 15 million passengers by 2012.

---

5   During this period tourism was actually more badly affected in Luxor and Aswan and it was during this period that many established tourist enterprises from these cities moved to Sharm El Sheikh, particularly jewellery shops.

6   While the breakdown of the Israeli–Palestinian peace process and recent bomb attacks have drastically reduced numbers of Israeli tourists from the Sinai in recent years, there are a few notable exceptions – day visitors to the casino in Taba, Israeli Palestinians (Arabs of 1948) in Dahab and Sharm El Sheikh and a determined minority of Israelis who frequent the beach camps in Nuweiba and Dahab.

Figure 3.1   Na'ama Bay, Sharm El Sheikh

Source: Jessica Jacobs 2003.

The visitor to Sharm El Sheikh can now find a large (ever expanding) modern tourist resort spread out along over 35km of coast, with many bars, nightclubs, over 50 diving centres and more than a 100 three to five star luxury hotels run by transnational corporations such as the *Hilton, Sonesta,* and *Four Seasons.* Many of these resorts can cover hundreds of acres of land – all-inclusive gated luxurious hotels with villa and apartment complexes and even their own transport systems.

Sexing the Sinai

Egypt has been a favoured destination with European men for ethnosexual encounters since the nineteenth century, a development of its occupation by French and British forces (Hopwood 2000). In recent years its popularity as a homosexual tourist-sex destination has declined due to the increasingly heavy-handed response from the Egyptian government with accounts of Egyptian men being imprisoned, raped and beaten when caught with foreign male tourists.[7] While the country is

---

7   The website www.gayegypt.com advises the following: 'Warning: Gay sex or any homosexual activity in Egypt puts you at risk of arrest, deportation or imprisonment and

probably now considered too socially conservative by heterosexual Western male sex tourists, the commercial selling of sex to male clients from Russia, Egypt and the Gulf (mostly by women from Russia and former Soviet countries) is not uncommon in tourist resorts like Sharm El Sheikh and Hurghada.[8]

Year-round sunshine, low prices and easy accessibility are definite factors in Sinai's attractiveness as a holiday destination. Return charter flights taking two to five hours are easily available from many European cities and a seven-day package including four- or five-star hotel accommodation can cost anything from €400–900 depending on the time of year. When they arrive, female tourists will discover that most 'locals' are men. Men, who have themselves travelled from the urban centres of Sinai, Egypt and even Sudan, to work in the booming tourist economy. Men who are, as we shall see, nevertheless imagined through this localness to be authentic and belonging to the Sinai environment and landscape.[9]

I first visited the Sinai in 1985 as a gap year student and soon noticed its popularity with other Western women. I also noticed how many of the ethnic encounters that took place between these women and local men became sexual encounters. Indeed many women quickly (after just a few days into their holiday) entered into ethnosexual relationships with a wide range of local men. Moreover the women involved returned to the Sinai and while many of these ethnosexual encounters became long-term relationships, others became the first of a series of different sexual encounters, a development I was able to note because I, too, returned on several occasions between 1993 and 1995, on breaks while working as a journalist in East Jerusalem and the West Bank, and later, in 1999 when I spent several months in the Sinai working for the travel guide book *Rough Guide: Egypt.*

I thus began this research with the premise that the diversity of these romantic and/or sexual ethnic encounters defied such a narrow definition as 'sex tourism', and a much broader context was needed. For my fieldwork, I chose the tourist resorts Sharm El Sheikh, Nuweiba and Dahab where the majority of tourist-local encounters took place. Over four months in 2000 I conducted 57 interviews with Western heterosexual tourist women and local men, most of who were (or had been) engaged in what Nagel (2003) has termed tourist-local ethnosexual relationships. I used a mixture of approaches from being introduced through mutual friends and acquaintances to approaching people directly while they were sunbathing on beaches and eating in cafes. My methodology was designed to work around my

---

any sexual encounter is undertaken at your own risk'. See later comments on the state's fear of the feminisation of Egyptian men.

8   For male sex tourists from the Gulf states, Egypt (particularly the cities of Cairo and Alexandria) has a reputation for being relatively accommodating when it comes to heterosexual sex outside of marriage (see El Gawhary 1995, Wynn 2007).

9   It is rare for women in Egypt to work in jobs that require them to live so far away from their homes except in contract employment in professional positions in four and five star hotels. However this is changing and an increasing number of men who work in the Sinai are relocating there with their families.

shifting positionality as a Western (tourist) woman who was also a frequent visitor and part-time resident.[10] Therefore, there was often an assumption by the women that I understood, if not participated in, their worldview. With the men, as well as my more obvious positionality as a Western woman on her own (so potentially someone they could have a sexual relationship with) I was also referenced as a 'local' in that I was also a part-time Sinai resident. All interviews were conducted in 'tourist English'[11] which was often the language of the relationship (sometimes a second language for both parties).

Most of the women I interviewed came from prosperous Western European countries such as Italy, the UK, Germany, Denmark and Switzerland, although several came from the United States. They varied in age (from 18 to 67), socio-economic origin and kind of holiday they were involved in (from a seven-day organised package to six months round the world backpacking to annual retreats). By opting to use in-depth interviews, I wanted to focus on their personal narratives rather than categorise them into different behavioural groups as some studies have attempted. In many ways the interviews were another form of encounter for the tourist/traveller and they always took place in the same spaces as other tourist encounters (including those leading to relationships and sex) such as the beach, the poolside, the hotel or the camp 'Bedouin tent'. In order to protect people's privacy, I avoided interviewing both partners unless they suggested it to me. All names have been changed to ensure anonymity.

On the Margins of Modernity: Paradise Beach and Empty Desert

According to Pollock, (Western) modernity appears to 'uproot, deracinate, detraditionalise' society making it difficult, if not impossible, to have a sense of belonging; except through 'a migration in time and space backwards to the premodern pasts' (1994: 66).

In the West travel – at least to places seen to exist outside of its borders – is often presented as symptom of this desire to belong, indulged in by the 'modern subject' (Oakes 2005, Minca and Oakes 2006) and fuelled by a nostalgic search for 'home' (Veijola 2006). In reference to MacCannell's (1976) definition of the tourist as a symbol of modernity's search for authenticity, Oakes suggests this can be taken further if definitions of the modern subject aren't limited to the mobility of the traveller/tourist; but understood in the places of encounter 'where traveller

---

10   My visits to the Sinai were most often from Palestine and other areas of the Middle East so I tended to view Sharm El Sheikh as very Western in comparison. However most of the women I interviewed arrived in the Sinai from Europe and North America and their positionality definitely influenced their idea of these resorts as representative of the 'Orient'

11   The men's shift pattern of work helped me to obtain interviews with many of the men because they often had several hours a day with little or nothing to do.

**Figure 3.2   The 30,000m² 'lazy river' water park and lush gardens of the
Jolie Ville Maritim Golf and Resort are typical of the extent
luxury hotels go to in order to produce a generic paradise
regardless of the desert surroundings**

Source: Jessica Jacobs (2010).

and 'other' meet and are forced to negotiate the meaning of the place in which they
find themselves.' (2005: 36) Thus, the 'seduction' of travel is not necessarily in the
movement, or travel itself, but the 'seduction of place'. Crouch also suggests that
'what the tourist does is a process of seductive encounter' (2005: 23).

In the case of a visit to Sinai – a desert in Egypt lodged between North Africa
and Southwest Asia and inhabited by a mostly Arab population – the seductive
encounter that takes place is with the 'Orient', and an Orient that has held a
particular place in European imaginations for several centuries. As Said notes:

> The Orient is not only adjacent to Europe; it is also the place of Europe's greatest
> and richest and oldest colonies, the source of its deepest and most recurring
> images of the Other. In addition the Orient has helped to define Europe (or the
> West) as its contrasting image, idea, personality, experience (1978, 1–2).

Thus the borders being crossed by these women travellers and tourists are not just
spatial, from fertile plain to desert mountains, from the hell of work to the paradise
of leisure, but also temporal, from the hectic busy now to a place that is far back in
time (Victorian to Biblical and beyond). The target landscapes of beach paradise
and desert retreat are accessed through a space of modernity seemed 'ultramodern'
(the airports and luxury hotels of the resorts), yet these demarcations are expressed

through the binaried construction of the Sinai as a series of opposites to modernity – a kind of anti-modernity (particularly in Dahab and Nuweiba), a pre-modernity and an un-modernity.

The Paradise Beach

As a landscape of stark contrast to Europe, the Sinai certainly has seductive powers. The mountainous interior is edged by a coast of coral-rich seas, lined by long stretches of date-palm beaches[12] and inhabited by homosocial images of the Other. The hotel resorts that cover the coast overtly appeal to a generic (global/tropical-inspired) image of paradise (See Figure 3.2). Against the contrasting backdrop of desert mountains, hotel outlets often add a décor that references a regional (rather than specific) tourist colonial nostalgia[13] of nineteenth-century Cairo or big game hunting in Africa (see Figure 3.3).

In the world of Western holidays the geographical imagination of paradise is more often than not deemed tropical and island-based. We are all familiar with images of empty white sandy beaches, palm trees, endless sunshine, exotic cocktails served by friendly brown-skinned natives. This tourist landscape is also the one most commonly associated with female sex tourism – particularly in the Caribbean. The Sinai of course is a desert, which does not fit the usual image of paradise, but thanks to its tropical coral reefs, palm trees (date, not coconut), sandy beaches, year-round sunshine and friendly natives, it can easily appropriate the imagery to suit the expectations and tastes of its visitors. It is not strictly speaking an island either, but as a peninsula it is sufficiently surrounded by sea and far enough away from large population centres to be experienced as one. Beach holidays in Egypt are a relatively new field compared with heritage (cultural) tourism in Luxor, Aswan and Cairo.

Ultramodern Sinai

Beach tourism in Egypt in general and in Sinai in particular is marketed very differently to the more established tourist sites. The Egyptian Tourist Authority's 2002 advertising campaign, for example, in the weekend supplements of the UK broadsheet press stresses the modernity of the Sinai facilities and can be said to be an attempt to position (and re-brand) Egypt in a market place dominated by other resorts in the Mediterranean and Caribbean. The expected imagery is there – the Pyramids of Cairo and the feluccas of the Nile in Aswan and Luxor – but these relics of the past are topped off with the 'ultra-modern' Red Sea, a perfect

---

12   Due to the lack of a local water source, most of the palm trees in Sharm El Sheikh are imported.

13   For a discussion of colonial nostalgia, see Peleggi (2005) and Bell (2005).

position from which to view this past. The resorts of the Sinai are 'pristine', 'lush' and full of 'friendly, welcoming staff'. The south of France is evoked by referring to the coast as a 'Riviera', while the abundance of palm trees and coral reefs place Egypt in the tropical destination bracket; Egypt is no longer confined to the limitations of the cultural heritage tourist market.

The beach resort tourism in the Sinai, has, from its inception in the 1990s, been allied with a Western generic tourist model of a tropical Caribbean paradise or the beaches of the Mediterranean rather than something especially Middle Eastern. Indeed the actual location of the Sinai in an Arab and predominantly Muslim country is not only a potential source of conflict with the tourist imaginary of a beach of freedom, tanning and casual sex, but can also cause real conflicts between a conservative Muslim population and a scantily-clad beach-going European.

Although paradise has previously been more closely linked to religious concepts, its literal Greek definition – a 'walled enclosure' – makes it an appropriate metaphor for much of modern tourism, taking place as it does within the walled enclosures of hotel compounds. In the emotional geography of place, the location of paradise is important. Like the desert, paradise (and its beaches) also has to be located away from the centre, on the margins.

For Nora, a young Swiss woman now living in a beach hut in Nuweiba with her Bedouin husband, the Sinai met all these requirements from the first moment she saw it.

> First time I come here, I feel I'm in paradise (Nora, 32, Nuweiba, April 2000).

Paola, a 33-year-old from Italy, has been visiting Sharm El Sheikh two to three times a year since she was in her early twenties. An avid tanner, her boyfriend at the time of the interview was Egyptian, a musician who played at the hotel where she stayed. It was love at first sight (and sense) for her, with the Sinai:

> When I got off the plane and the heat hit me and I saw the mountains – I fell in love with the Sinai (Paola, 33, Sharm El Sheikh, April 2000).

Glossy brochures advertising the resorts of the Sinai, particularly Sharm El Sheikh, feature holidays similar to any number of packages on offer in other beach resorts around the world that model themselves as paradise, such as the Caribbean, the Seychelles and Thailand. Despite the desert location and extreme water shortage, lush, landscaped gardens reminiscent of the Western idea of the 'garden paradise', full of palm trees, waterfalls and tropical flowers have become the norm.

While some hotels are small, manager-owned enterprises that stress the locality by taking their names from local sources, the majority of the larger resort hotels

Figure 3.3   The bar at the Meridien/Savoy attempts to conjure up an image of a colonial Africa of big game hunting with 'colonial' furniture and paintings of elephants and lions

Source: Jessica Jacobs (2001).

have taken on a generic globalised image, giving the tourist the impression that a certain experience is on offer regardless of the actual country specifics. Thus international hotel brands such as the *Sonesta, Hilton, Intercontinental* and *Four Seasons* are all there with names that attempt to reinforce globalised geographical imaginaries of tropical paradises with names such as *Royal Paradise, Dreams Beach, Mexicana, Hilton Dreams, Hilton Waterfalls* and *Tropicana*. This kind of naming is also extended to the different outlets at the hotel, so restaurants and bars also refer back to combined imaginations of paradise, deserts and colonial heydays.

The *Meridien,* a large resort hotel in Sharm El Sheikh now managed by the *Savoy*, has decorated its outlets in styles that are typical of this mixture of themes. In particular this can be seen in its colonial nostalgic themed bar, decorated as an African safari outpost with zebra skin sofas (not real), rattan armchairs and large oil paintings of elephants and tigers on the wall, harking back to an era of big game hunting. Other bars appeal to the idea of a 'Latin' or Caribbean themed nightlife, such as the *Mexican Bar, Calypso* and *Salsa.*

The Unmodern

While Egyptian visitors might look upon the beach resorts of the Sinai as a symbol of their country's embrace of modernity, the same resorts are also imagined as proof of Egypt's perceived lack of modernity. Resorts like Sharm El Sheikh might be 'ultra-modern' but this modernity is usually perceived as belonging to transnational global corporations rather than being homegrown. Moreover the modern facilities of the Red Sea resorts such as diving centres and hotels in their brochures, are all too often perceived has having been primarily designed for a Western clientele (an idea reinforced by being paid for in foreign rather than local currencies) reinforcing an idea of a Western rather than Egyptian modernity.

For Gertrude and Caroline, two married German women in their fifties (one of whom was engaged in a friendship with a young Egyptian man) the five-star hotel resorts of Sharm El Sheikh were a refuge of modernity symbolising Western values. They were visiting Sharm El Sheikh on a two week package holiday and told me they chose their hotel because, flicking through the various brochures in the travel agents, they spotted a photo of a hotel perched on top of a cliff that had an elevator to take guests to the beach below. It was this lift they said, that made them choose to come to Sharm El Sheikh – a reassuring emblem of modernity in an unknown 'un-modern' country.

> JJ: *The first time you came, what made you decide to come? What was the ...?*
> Gertrude: It's a nice story. We wanted to go to Sri Lanka, but we look in the catalogue and then I say 'Ah, we can go to Sinai', and then we don't know a nice place, then we see one nice with the elevator here and then I think of course I read was Hilton before and I think when there was Hilton before it's a nice place, very nice looking and then I see this elevator and I say come let's try Caroline, we'll go there and we'll take this hotel. So we be right! (Gertrude, 58, Sharm El Sheikh, April 2000).

Another major element in the construction of the Sinai as a site outside of modernity was its cheapness in relation to Europe. Sinai is generally considered to be a cheap (or good value) destination whether the product you purchase is a luxury hotel package, or budget backpacker camping. Sharm El Sheikh in particular is seen to combine a cheap holiday (it is outside Europe) with luxury facilities promised by the international standards of a *Hilton* (or a least a former *Hilton*).

Modernity, especially its more luxurious infrastructural elements, is not expected to be cheap but most tourists travelling to resorts outside of the West expect prices to be significantly lower. The expectation of cost is split definitively along 'modern' and 'unmodern' lines. The costs of hotel accommodation and scuba diving courses for example are expected to be cheaper than if consumed in Europe, but they are still considered Western products and priced in dollars or Euros to reflect this, as if they are imported goods. However the cost of what are seen to be local commodities are expected to be significantly lower.[14] A trip to Sharm El Sheikh is selected because visitors hope to get a paradise that offers the best of both 'worlds'– a veneer at least of modernity, at a thoroughly unmodern price.

This conceptualisation is maintained despite the relative sophistication of resorts like Sharm el Sheikh, because the infrastructure is tourist infrastructure, designed mostly for Europeans and as such represents Western modernity, albeit with an 'exotic' flavour. It is a little piece of home – a place of safety the tourist and traveller has from which to venture out.

Inevitably this conceptualisation of Sinai as a paradisial combination of the 'un-modern' and 'modern' leads to tensions and disappointment. What is modern and what isn't does not always favour the needs and desires of the consumer. Gertrude and her friend were particularly indignant at the high price of alcohol, which was on a par with the price they would pay at a hotel in Germany.

> Really the price of drinks here are too expensive!…Yes you would pay this in a
> hotel in Europe, but this isn't Europe! It is not the same… (Gertrude, 58, Sharm
> El Sheikh, April 2000).

The Desert Retreat

While paradise, at least the beach version, has long been accepted as holding a strong appeal for women, the desert, as Massey points out, has a 'long history… not just of the exclusion of women but of the contested constitution of what it was going to *mean to be* a (certain kind of) man and woman' (2005: 144). For centuries they have represented a space of sanctuary for those disaffected with political systems and cultures; more recently they have appealed to colonial European travellers (Lindqvist 2002) and, as a metaphor at least, to poststructural theorists.

Colonial European travellers, theorists on modernity (and, it would appear, European women tourists) all give the desert – and the Bedouin – a special role in their emotional imaginative geographies of place. As an supposedly empty place, yet capable of sustaining life if you know where to look. It has long been considered the antithesis of civilisation and is also associated with metaphysical qualities – fasting in the desert (as a representation of the withdrawal from the material world) was an important component of the life and teachings of Jesus that has been absorbed into Western (Christian) culture.

A *Guardian* book review of the re-publication of *Deserts* (Dyer 2001), suggests that the desert is a relative newcomer as an aesthetic ideal of landscape. Indeed, the Western world has shown relatively little interest in the desert except during the

---

14   It is not uncommon for visitors to resorts in Sinai to pay a diving centre over €400 for a diving course without blinking or bargaining, then argue with a taxi driver over a €2 fare, or haggle over the price of a €4 pair of trousers or a €8 hotel room if the product is deemed to be 'local'.

Crusades and the colonising late nineteenth and early twentieth centuries. It was here, at the turn into the last century, that the desert began to attain a grandeur and importance with its 'weird solitude, the great silence, the grim desolation' and most importantly a belief that it was a 'manifestation of the sublime' (Dyer 2001).

The revival of interest in deserts during late colonialism and the establishment of modernity is no coincidence. Lindqvist (2000) notes how irresistible the desert was to angst-ridden late nineteenth-century European writers such as Pierre Loti who saw the desert as a place where time has stopped:

> In the desert all changes have already occurred. Nothing grows, nothing dies, nothing decays. Everything has gone. Only eternity remains (2000: 68).

The use of the desert by Western postmodern theorists as a site of what Kaplan calls 'philosophical epiphany' (1998) has been of lasting appeal. Kaplan has not only noted the masculinized nature of the modern subject, but how, for writers such as Baudrillard[15] and Jean Philippe Mathy.[16] the arid landscape of the desert has been co-opted into a Western confrontation with humanism and modernity and therefore presents an 'opportunity for Euro-American inventions of the self' (1998: 66).

For Bauman the significance of the desert goes well beyond that of mere geographical area or landscape, its supposed emptiness allows it to be a 'land of self-creation' and represents 'raw, bare, primal and bottom-line freedom' (1996: 20).

> The desert meant putting a distance between oneself and one's duties and obligations...The desert...was a land not yet sliced into places, and for that reason it was a land of self-creation (1996: 20).

According to Kaplan in the European imaginary, the desert signifies a 'loss of bearings, the absence of any permanent marks of modern civilisation, and the experience of literal dis-orientation' which is then used in the Western confrontation with humanism and modernity; while its inhabitants, the Bedouin, symbolise 'a subject position that offers an idealized model of movement based on perpetual displacement' (1998: 64).

This discourse on the desert tends to rely upon the continued romanticisation and theorisation of travel, which Kaplan argues builds 'essentialist entities' through mystical metaphysics 'that function in binary opposition to one another' (1998: 69). However, as she points out, 'the desire to become like or merge with the periphery or margin that one's own power has established demonstrates the pitfalls of theoretical tourism' (1998: 67).

---

15   See also Pels (1999).

16   Kaplan is referring to the work of Jean-Phillipe Mathy (1993), *Extreme-Occident: French Intellectuals and America*.

The desert as a non-place, and therefore somewhere to go to escape from a place, is a recurring and of course paradoxical theme. While mystified versions of the romance of the desert remain with us, often in the supposed service of postcolonial critical practice, Kaplan argues that instead they produce, 'a postmodern discourse of displacement that relies upon a host of Euro-American modernist tropes: exile, solitude, distance, emptiness, nostalgia, and loss' (1998: 69).

Kaplan points out that these postmodern discourses cannot be separated from the dominant Orientalisms that have been circulating throughout modernity. Writing a place as 'empty' allows for colonisation with the coloniser accorded sovereign subject status.

Indeed, if the male colonising travel writer helped to create landscapes as 'empty' in order for them to be filled with Western colonial projects, the postmodern anxiety about the endless onslaught of modernity would seem to have more in common with the writing of the Victorian and Edwardian women who travelled, and who as Birkett points out, were often more concerned than men with keeping somewhere untouched by modernity – so they would remain 'uncivilised' for the purposes of maintaining an escapist retreat.

For some holidaymakers in Sinai, the desert is just a pleasant (or even unpleasant) backdrop to their package sun and sea holiday; for others it is the reason they are there and these women often head straight for Dahab and Nuweiba as soon as they get off the plane to stay in Bedouin-run camps on the coast or to go on a 'safari' in the desert, rather than settle for the bright lights and built-up hotels of Sharm El Sheikh.

Today the Sinai has become a desert where Europeans and North Americans come to search for freedom, to experience a place that remains untouched by modernity (to a degree at least). In particular when this freedom is associated with its desert environment, the imaginative landscape is of a desert that is premodern and/or 'antimodern'.

Karen, an 40-year-old American freelance photographer, has been dividing her life between her New York studio and a small house in the Bedouin village of Asilah (Dahab) for the last 20 years, which also doubles as a gallery space for her Bedouin portraits and desert landscapes. For Karen, life in the Sinai was the 'opposite' of her busy hectic and trapped urban life in New York:

> Sinai is important because it embodies freedom…For me that was the attraction.
> I love the wilderness but as a single woman I can't approach it. So for me Sinai
> was the approachable wilderness. Sinai itself has come to mean to me a symbol
> of freedom (Karen, 40, Dahab, September 2000).

Marianne was a 39-year old former special needs teacher from Germany when I met her. She first came to the Sinai with her German boyfriend in the early 1990s. She has since returned on several occasions to Dahab and later to Nuweiba but each time entering into a new relationship with a local man. For her the relationship was primarily with the Sinai.

> The first time I came here, the feeling was, now I can die. I felt really released...It
> was a very, very big feeling very strong (Marianne, 39, Nuweiba, April 2000).

Luisa, 42, from Germany, has been visiting the Sinai every year for 12 years. She
is married with two children but always comes alone. Every year she books into
the only Bedouin-run hotel in Sharm El Sheikh where she contacts her favourite
Bedouin guides who take her to live in the desert for five to six days. She returns
to the hotel and then back to Germany. The desert, according to Luisa, is the only
place she has found where she can truly be alone (except of course for her male
Bedouin guides) and feel she has escaped her duties as a wife and mother back
in Germany. Luisa is not the only woman who does this. According to Jamal, a
Bedouin guide who also works at the Bedouin-run hotel, this is a common request.
Especially among European women in their thirties and forties and above. Despite
the predominantly male postmodern preoccupation with empty deserts and ideas
of the modern subject, in the Sinai at least, it is mostly women, not men, who
request to be taken into the interior by Bedouin men, and ask to be left there, only
to be visited occasionally with food and water supplies.

   The desert is seen as a hopelessly romantic idea, something Lindqvist (2000)
ascribes to 'emptiness of its space, the barrenness of its ground' and most of all
its silence:

> At last a silence which is never broken in a desolate country where no one comes
> and no one goes. Strangely the same silence seems so threatening in the town...
> (2000: 51).

Several of the women I interviewed mentioned this combined quality of silence
and safety when describing the desert – something that was felt to be missing
in (or opposite to) Europe or North America. Astrid, a 46-year-old woman from
Germany said she would normally be afraid to be a woman alone in Europe,
especially at night. But in the desert she felt safe:

> I'm much more afraid to be in the night in the main station in Munich or in
> Frankfurt like I sleep all night in the desert here (Astrid, 46, Dahab, September
> 2000).

Premodern

Just as Pollock says of modernity's longing for a home seen to be only accessible
through a migration back in time, the Sinai has come to symbolise a version of
premodernity to many women through a variety of imaginative geographies of its
desert and paradise. Here the Sinai, rich in the premodern religious history of the
Bible and the Pharaoahs of 'Antiquity', is a landscape accessed as such through
the concomitant imagining the contemporary inhabitants as premodern primitives,

something I will explore in more detail in the next chapter. This, then is very different from a simple absence of modernity, a journey to the Sinai here is not just to a lack of the modern, but to a place and time *before* modernity; a visit to the Sinai is a form of time travel accompanied by a strong sense of nostalgia for a time that has passed elsewhere.

The Sinai has many historical religious associations; it is considered to be the birthplace of monotheism, the site recorded in Judeo-Christian and Muslim culture where the Jews wandered for 40 years and where Moses received the Ten Commandments. In the Christian New Testament, Jesus is also supposed to have passed through on his 'Flight to Egypt'. It is also the location, along with Egypt's Eastern desert, of the first desert monastery, a form of Christian organisation that spread to Europe only centuries later. A significant proportion of Sinai tourists travel to specifically climb Mount Sinai and visit St Catherine's Monastery because of these Biblical imaginations, and even if visitors are not aware of this association before they arrive, all tour operators offer this trip as a day excursion from every hotel. Aside from these religious historical associations, as we have seen in Western culture and narratives of modernity, the desert landscape is (perhaps more than any other landscape) presented as somehow 'frozen in time'. This can lead to attempts to read the landscape as still representing a past time, in this case a spiritual past that existed prior to the onset of modernity and somehow still manages to exist alongside modernity in the landscape of the Sinai and in the lives of its Bedouin inhabitants.

As Bernal (1991) and others have pointed out, the search for 'origins', both physical and metaphysical, is a major motif of modernity, a desire that has gave impetus to countless (colonial and other) voyages of exploration. Many searches get forgotten only to resurface later in response to political and cultural developments. The creation of the state of Israel in 1948 has had a great effect on the Sinai in this regard, influencing and providing tourists (both Christian and Jewish) with religiously themed holidays. For many of the women I interviewed it was hard for them to separate the imagined premodernity of the Sinai and its people from their ethnosexual encounters.

Steffanie, 26, from Switzerland, was a devout 22-year-old Christian when she first visited Sinai. She told me she had come because she wanted to see the actual place where Moses had received the Ten Commandments that she had read so much about. Her emotional geography of this desert landscape was romantic certainly but this romance was expressed in spiritual terms:

> I didn't know a lot about Sinai when I was in Switzerland. I saw some films about the monastery of St Catherine. And it impressed me I remember this now. And I imagined that I would live in this area. But I remember that I saw this film and it impressed me – this area and these mountains and this silence and also this mystic atmosphere, the history also. It was somehow impressive for me because (of) the religion – most of the big religions are here (Steffanie, 26, Dahab, April 2000).

After arriving in Cairo however, Steffanie met some travellers who recommended Dahab to her as a good and cheap place to stay in the Sinai. She immediately liked the atmosphere, telling me:

> Everyone you meet people talking about religion. So it was for me a place of secrets and it made me just curious... (Steffanie, 26, Dahab, April 2000).

One of these people was a local man who was Muslim, already married and 16 years older than her. A week later she married him, became a Muslim and after several months set up a business with her husband managing a small budget hotel. Steffanie's geographical imagination of the Sinai has given it a hyper-religiosity of meaning, a premodern landscape of Biblical proportions. But, as I will explore further in the next chapter, it was only through her marriage to a local that she was able to stay in the Sinai in a way that satisfied her desire to access this imagination. Doing 'as the locals do', she also adopted the local religion:

> Yes, it's nice because when you get really into this religion, you enjoy it. You start to enjoy it – to feel that you have a way to get closer to God. And this was always my aim, because I see this world and I see this nature and I know there must be some power who did all this (Steffanie, 26, Dahab, April 2000).

Sonja, 50, from Germany, is a mother of two, and before she came to the Sinai in the early 1990s she used to manage a restaurant in a German lake resort with her German husband. On her first visit she met a much younger Egyptian man and later divorced her husband to marry him and move to the Sinai where she now owns and manages a camp for scuba divers. She told me she fell in love with the Sinai before she fell in love with her new husband.

> I make a holiday in Israel and I booked a diving safari to Sinai. And I always think it was the moment I lost my heart in Sinai you know. The feeling you know, the sun, the mountains, the Bedouins are there, they (are) very nice at this time. So it was for me a special feeling you know. So this was the time that I can really enjoy you know. There is (sic) no tourists in this area (Sonja, 50, Dahab, September 2000).

Sonja initially visited the Sinai to scuba dive in the Red Sea, an activity first made popular by Jacques Cousteau in the 1950s. Scuba diving is heavily dependent on technology – you need complicated breathing apparatus, special material in the diving suits, specific courses run by accredited Western organisations – to gain access to the underwater world of coral reefs and tropical fish. All in all, and considering it requires the belief that humans can overcome inhospitable environments, it is a very modern activity. It is also an activity that you can participate in just up the coast in the ultramodern Israeli resort of Eilat. Yet the Sinai – so close to Israel and Europe, yet on the margins – not too far to be too strange, and not too far to feel completely displaced from your home, is perceived differently to Eilat. It is still a 'wilderness' and still populated with friendly hospitable natives. Here Sonja comments on the differences between the modern Europe/Israel and the pre and unmodern Sinai and why she prefers the latter:

> I travelled after this a lot in Israel and I come three times with the car from Germany through Israel to Sinai you know. But it's a totally different feeling – I mean (in Israel and Europe) – nobody helps you, nobody saying something to you. So different here…the contact was much more faster to the people. Especially here in Dahab and I sit with the Bedouins and everything like this you know. So anyway the Sinai is for me more interesting because everything is very close. You have here the sea, and if I walk out half an hour, I can be totally alone in any mountain here…I start to love this place (Sonja, 50, Dahab, September 2000).

Eilat is just over 100km north of Dahab. It sits at the foot of the same desert mountains looking over the same sea, with the same coral reefs, yet diving in Eilat is not considered as desirable as diving in the Sinai. The alienating modernity of Eilat means that there is no 'closeness' with nature, a closeness that is attainable in Dahab with its low-key backpacker tourism, a closeness that can be accessed through the 'friendly' Bedouin inhabitants.

The idea of a different 'time' in Sinai applies to the sense of history that the desert evokes, especially among the geographical imaginations of the European visitor. It is premodern in this sense but also in the rhythm of life of the people who live there. The Sinai is seen to offer the tourist and traveller a different time to that of the west, a time out from the stress of the city and modern life. For Sonja, it was the different rhythm of time that contributed to her losing her heart in the Sinai, that gave her the sense she had left modernity for this other 'time' populated by the premodern Bedouin.

> Also I have a feeling like…I don't know how to explain, but my heart opened you know. It was like – actually I'd run away from the stress and from too much work in Germany you know…I see the Bedouins – these people that live long time here – but I doesn't (sic) talk one word Arabic in this time. I don't want, you know, I just want to enjoy my time. To relax from Germany you know. And the life, it was…I mean it's (a) hard life sometimes here, of course, when you have business you know. But in the same time it goes everything a step slower you know from the rush that we know (Sonja, 50, Dahab, September 2000).

Modernity then, is fast moving, stressful and focuses on work, while premodernity involves a much slower, more relaxed tempo. You can fly to the Sinai in a matter of hours, but once you are there you can sit in a café and wait the same amount of time for a cup of tea.

Modernity is also seen as a condition of being surrounded by other people. You can only be alone in open spaces, woodlands, the countryside, the few designated 'wildernesses' that are left in Europe. For many women, these wildernesses are often linked to ideas of vulnerability, danger and the threat of attack by men. However a premodern Sinai helped women to feel safe and allowed them to experience 'space' by themselves and in safety, protected of course by their privileged position as tourists among other factors.

At first glance this benign view of the Sinai seems strange when it has been the focus of recent bomb attacks (Dahab in April 2006 and Sharm El Sheikh in June 2005) and seems to contradict many other (dominating) imaginations of the Middle East as an 'unsafe' destination for single women. Yet as we have seen, numbers of visitors to the region have continued to increase substantially year on year, a sign perhaps of the strength of conviction that Sinai exists outside of modernity and is not temporally connected to contemporary Middle Eastern society with all its social and political complexities.

Anti-modern

The idea of emptiness (apart from friendly natives) and its association with safety was very strong among many women, particularly those from Germany such as Susanne, 52, Rita, 37 and Ursula, 29. This narrative was just one of many that constructed Sinai as an opposite to Western Europe and North America and offered this as the reason why Sinai was so attractive – it was the antithesis of modernity and could therefore help these women express their antimodernity. When Steffanie, the young Swiss woman who runs a hotel in Dahab, described the impact of the Sinai on her guests she also focused on the supposed emptiness of the desert and in doing so, firmly positioned the desert as both an opposite of crowded Europe, but also the adjacent Red Sea:

> There is no green, there is no plants, no vegetation so you feel it's a big contrast between the desert and under the water. It's like a garden, it's like the opposite. In Switzerland you have green and gardens and much life and under the water there is not much life. And here it's the opposite. You sit in an area without green, without a lot of animals not like we know it and then you go under the water and you find all these animals and all these colours and it's very impressive, it's very beautiful (Steffanie, 26, Dahab, April 2000).

Nora, 32, was a former student nurse from Switzerland. She first came to the Sinai with a group of friends but soon returned on her own to marry her Bedouin boyfriend from that holiday. She now lives with him in the desert and has adopted what she interprets to be the dress and customs of 'traditional' Bedouin society. They have three sons. Nora also focused on the oppositeness of the Sinai in comparison to her life in Switzerland. Sinai was a paradise-desert, and the absence of civilisation allowed her to have a direct contact with Nature.

> What I really like here is to be very close to the nature. And with the fire (We are sitting around a fire). And with the wind. With the water. With the earth. Everyday I have really contact, really. This I don't have in Switzerland. For me it's more easy to live. ...I get all the power from the nature and I think this... how I live is really a dream of everyone, everyone (Nora, 32, Nuweiba, April 2000).

For Nora moving to the Sinai has provided the solution to her disillusionment with Europe. She has 'time' and she lives in 'nature' – a style of life that she believes is a common 'dream' in the modern West.

Conclusion

In the tourist imaginary the desert and paradise share many qualities. They are both located away from the centre – on the margins both geographically and in terms of time. As Wilson says of tourist 'paradise' in Hawaii, they are thought of as 'out-of history' (1994: 40). However while the facilities that accompany the beach paradise allow it to be marketed as belonging to an ultra-modernity, the desert tends to remain a site firmly rooted in the (colonial/Biblical) past.

Today the Sinai is also famous for its scuba diving opportunities in the Red Sea and its beaches, which draw upon other imaginations of tropical island paradises. However, whether the tourist is travelling to Sinai for its coastline or the desert landscape, much of the draw for the tourist is heavily based on the tourist's imagination of the colonial experience of the Middle East and geographical imaginations of paradise and deserts that have been filtered through literary and cinematic imageries; imaginaries that are used to sell the Sinai as a tourist destination.

Desert imaginaries have also been influenced by the use of deserts as a symbol for displacement, exile and disillusionment with modernity by postmodern theorists. In their interviews, women frequently spoke of finding paradise *and* freedom in the Sinai, whether on the beach or in the desert (or both). Indeed, their emotional attachment to place – to the landscape – seemed inextricably tied up with ideas of paradise and Bauman's desert of 'freedom' and 'land of self-creation'. This attachment was not only immediate, it was often expressed in stronger terms and seen to be longer lasting than the women's attraction to (specific) local men. It is important to note that geographical and historical imaginations are heavily gendered – in terms of what actual men and women do in the Sinai and what they have done in the past – and in more abstract terms of Western hegemonic notions of masculinity and femininity attached to the people and places of the Sinai. In addition the influence of these imaginations of the desert and the beach are not confined to Western tourists. Egyptian men who have migrated to the Sinai from the Nile Valley also have strong geographical imaginations of the desert and the beach, some of which have also been influenced by exposure to Western discourses on landscapes, places and people, and I will explore this further in Chapter 5.

European women are engaging their geographical and historical imaginations of tropical island paradise and/or the desert wilderness through the touristscapes of the Sinai; effectively constructing binaries that oppose the Sinai with the cities and civilisation they come from – pitting modernity against nature and wilderness and freedom, their supposed opposites.

These geographical imaginations can be all too brief and feel very superficial and inauthentic for many visitors, particularly when experienced through the tourist excursion, perhaps to participate for one hour in an re-enactment of a Bedouin 'tradition' like camel riding. Yet, as we shall see in the next chapter, the option of a romantic and/or sexual ethnic encounter with a local man allows women a way in – for these relationships offer the local as a guide, an interlocuter, an interpreter who allows these women to feel they are truly experiencing an encounter with an 'other'. Another landscape, another people, another time. This is achieved, or at least attempted, because men in the Sinai are also implicated in these geographical imaginations and through racial and sexual stereotyping are seen to embody ideas of masculinity, an absence of modernity, and a presence of nature and wilderness that accompany these imaginative geographies.

Karen's comments about freedom and safety also highlight a difference between the male modern romance with deserts such as the Sahara and the more female-friendly Sinai. Its combination of emptiness with facility-rich accessibility provides a safe 'modern' space from which women can explore their identities.

For, despite the predominantly masculine modern subjectivities that surround empty deserts, in the Sinai at least, it is mostly women, not men, who arrive by charter flight, meet up with their boyfriends/husbands (or find new ones) or just arrange for local Bedouin men to take them into the desert, for a few days or weeks so they can paint, photography or just contemplate the nature of modernity and create and consume their imagined routes to freedom.

Chapter 4
Becoming a Nomad – The Ethnosexual Encounter Today

Introduction

Western representations of the Orient are, aside from the geographical specificity of location, based on embodied difference. As Yegenoglu (2005) points out, these representations are most often articulated through the 'simultaneous gesture of racialization and feminization' (2005: 73).

Yet Said and others such as Gregory (1999, 2001) rarely refer to issues of gender (or women specifically) in their treatment of Orientalism. Indeed, it is only relatively recently that gendered approaches have been produced by Kabbani (1994), Lewis (1996), Garcia-Ramon, Albet-Mas, Nogue-Font and Riudor-Gorgas (1998), Dobie (2001), and Yegenoglu (2005).

Others, such as Stoler (1995) and Bhabha (1994) have also explored the role of race in the construction of colonial (racial) sexualities. However, when it comes to the Western preoccupation with 'Eastern' sexuality, women are perhaps over-represented. The most recurring image and motif of sex in the Orient is the harem and other fantasies of femininity (Grewal 1996, Alloula 1986, Croutier 1998, Hopwood 2000). Interestingly, when the Orient is associated with masculinity, the imagined, innate Arab traits include violence (Kabbani, below), masturbation (Said 1978: 316), pederasty (Boone 1995), homosociality (Ghassoub and Sinclair-Webb 2006) and perversion in general (Massad 2007).[1] Kabbani for example notes:

> In the European narration of the Orient, there was a deliberate stress on those qualities that made the East different from the West, exiled it into an irretrievable state of 'otherness'. Among the many themes that emerge from the European narration of the Other, two appear most strikingly. The first is the insistent claim that the East was a place of lascivious sensuality, and the second that it was a realm characterised by inherent violence (1994: 5–6).

The tendency to define othered landscapes in racialized and gendered terms is however, not just present in colonial discourse. As we have seen in Chapter 3, postmodern theorists that utilise the metaphor of the desert and desert-dwellers,

---

1 Massad (2007) argues that use of sexual humiliation as an interrogation technique in Guantanamo Bay and Abu Ghraib reflects the accumulation of centuries of Western assumptions about male Arab sexuality.

do so in order to create an opposite to modernity where the desert landscape and people of the Orient – are feminised and dualistically opposed to an essentialist (Western) masculine travelling subjectivity. In his commentary on the hero Porter Moresby in Paul Bowles 1949 novel *The Sheltering Sky*, Oakes (2005) discusses the double role of the desert in the Western imaginary of (post)modernity.

> While one might be tempted to argue that the desert is a purely symbolic landscape marking Port as a modern subject, it seems that Bowles' use of the desert goes far beyond its *symbolic* value in aiding the visualization of modernity's paradoxical subjectivity (2005).

Kaplan, notes how in Baudrillard's *America* (1988) he most consistently links the term 'woman' to landscape, 'in particular the "desert"' (1998: 77). Feminisation of landscapes contribute to their construction as 'empty', passive and therefore available to the dominant gaze of a paradoxical – but essentially masculine – subjectivity.

Oakes argues the desert shows itself to be so much more than a postmodern metaphor for paradoxical subjectivity in Bowles' *Sheltering Sky* because of its desert-dwelling 'Arab' inhabitants. Not only does their presence make the desert a 'real place', it becomes sexualised:

> Although it represents displacement and exile for Port, the desert is also *a real place*—a home to the other, the Arab. ... The Arabs are at home in the desert; their lives display the ceaseless motion that the desert itself displays and demands for survival. It is they who make the desert a place. And as a place, the desert offers more than backdrop and stage; it offers an *encounter with the other*. Encounter in place, more than movement and journey through space, is what articulates the subjectivity of paradox in *The Sheltering Sky*. And more than anything, the encounters between traveler and other in Bowles' novel are experienced as *seductions* (2005).

When it comes to desert-dwellers (real or imagined) — the relationship to race and gender is more complex than to landscape alone – and more problematic. For while Bedouins have been given what Beezer terms the 'burden of embodiment' (2003: 131) of this feminised landscape they have also been charged with embodying the array of essentialist Arab masculine traits mentioned above.

Indeed, the Arab Bedouin represents one of the recurring themes of modernity – but only as a man. Then he occupies what Kaplan calls 'a highly masculine subject position that offers an idealized model of movement based on perpetual displacement' (1998: 66). The male Western/modern subject, by appropriating this nomadic identity – by 'becoming nomad' – is exposed:

> This 'man' could also be seen as a construction of Euro-American prerogatives: 'central,' he visits the margins; 'empty', he recreates emptiness in the world around him; 'modern', he looks for an escape from modernity (1998: 73).

As we have seen, the position of the modern male subject is not only open to men. Western women have been adopting this subjectivity to travel in the global South from early modernity onwards. The sexualised, racialised and seductive appeal of place that Oakes notes in Bowles work is, perhaps left out of Kaplan's account of the postmodern obsession with deserts. For modern Western society in the shape of 'civilisation' (modernity) is, as Pasztory notes, often imagined as feminine, 'searching for that lost, masculine lover' (2001: 18). In the following chapter I will argue that the burden of embodiment can just as easily be placed upon the women who travel to the Sinai, as it can on the local men they become sexually and/or romantically involved with. Indeed the women's appropriation of the positionality of the modern male subject is crucial in their search for that lost, masculine lover among the 'perpetually displaced' nomads of the Sinai and shows that the seductive appeal of deserts and their homosocial inhabitants has never really been an exclusively Western male prerogative.

Desert Queens and Embodied Nomads

There is a significant strand of late colonial travel/writing and photography by women such as Gertrude Bell (1868–1926), Freya Stark (1893–1993) and Lady Lucie Duff Gordon (1821–1869) that has focused on deserts and their Arab inhabitants in the Middle East and North Africa. Many have had their work republished in recent years and their lives have been the focus of biographies with titles such as *Freya Stark: Passionate Nomad* (1999, 2001) and *The Desert Queen: The Extraordinary Life of Gertrude Bell* (1997) and *Gertrude Bell: Queen of the Desert, Shaper of Nations* (2008). While the romantic Orientalist aspect of their adventures are emphasised, titles like these also show how these adventurer explorers are presented today as women who challenged their own societal values. They also reflect the complexity of the women's relationship with the prevailing colonialist/Orientalist projects as explored in the work of Blunt (2005), Pratt (1992) and Mills (1991, 1996).

Unfortunately there has been little research to date on the ethnosexual encounters among Victorian and Edwardian women travellers aside from those such as Swiss-born Isabelle Eberhardt (1877–1904) and British-born Jane Digby (1807–1881) who married Arab men in Algeria and Syria respectively (see Littlewood 2001 and Lindqvist 2000). Yet awareness of 'passionate' women and their predilection for desert landscapes and nomadic men has not gone unnoticed in Western cultural production. Images of Arab men are nearly always sexualised in films such as *The Sheik* (dir. George Melford 1921), *Death on the Nile* (dir. John Guillermin 1978), *Lawrence of Arabia* (dir. David Lean 1962) and *Indiana Jones and the Last Crusade* (dir. Steven Spielberg 1989). While *Lawrence of Arabia* and *Indiana Jones* are also action movies aimed at a male audience; as Studlar (1997) points out, when Hollywood does Orientalisms, it is usually with a female audience in mind. Bach (1997) also notes how popular romantic fiction in the West first seized upon the motif of the handsome and exotic Arab sheikh in the desert in the 1920s and although this was eclipsed by war-time heroes in the 1940s, it has since returned to centre stage among such publishers as Mills and Boon. And even (to which I shall return later) in the Booker Prize-nominated novel, *The Map of Love* (1999) by Adhaf Soueif.

The marketing of holidays to countries like Egypt in contemporary Western society not only draws upon these romantic and nostalgic images, it reinscribes and reinforces them, encouraging tourists to turn them into tourist practice. The emphasis on intrepid Orientalist archaeological travellers (both male and female), costume and overt sensuality (the veil, the harem *and* the robes of Bedouin/Arab masculinity) and the (potential) freedom of the desert, are not just used to sell the destination, they also produce it.

According to Lindqvist 'in the spiritual life of Europe, the colonies had an important function – as a safety vent, as an escape, as a place to misbehave' (2000: 51). Lindqvist suggests that for Eberhardt (and also for Nobel Prize-winning author André Gide 1869–1951), the deserts of North Africa were 'primarily an erotic experience'. Certainly, if in the Western imaginary the desert is stable, never changing, this supposed emptiness allows for the placing of all sorts of imaginaries onto desert space. But crucially this desert also acts as a boundary for Europe and crossing it can mean crossing other boundaries too. Not only did the nineteenth century travellers Isabelle Eberhardt and Jane Digby marry Arab men, they lived in the desert and never returned to Europe. The boundaries they crossed were spatial, but also bound up in their gendered subjectivities of race, sex and religion. According to Lindqvist 'in the spiritual life of Europe, the colonies had an important function – as a safety vent, as an escape, a place to misbehave' (2000: 51). Lindqvist suggests that for Eberhardt and also the Nobel Prize winning author André Gide (1869–1951) the deserts of North Africa were 'primarily an erotic experience'.

Today the Sinai local can be a Bedouin, an Egyptian or even a European, but – aside from the hotel facilities – it is the Bedouin (and poorer Egyptians) who visually dominate the marketing literature thanks to their historicity and connection to the surrounding desert/palm tree oasis landscape. Their authenticity is represented by images showing them in traditional clothing and references to their customs, while their sexual availability is hinted at by the stress on 'native' traditions of welcoming hospitality (Beezer 1993, Jacobs 2003). The Bedouin inhabitants, excluded from any direct involvement with tourist development, are eulogised for their affinity with Nature and for the freedom of their supposedly wandering lifestyle, of always being 'on the move',[2] an identity that is inextricably linked with their masculinity, not only by Westerners, but internalised by many Bedouin themselves.

Beezer suggests that while an imaginary of the desert as a space for 'spiritual rebuilding' is a common motif in many cultures, the 'othering' of this desert landscape (and people), is unique to Western sensibilities.

---

2   Bedouins were 'pastoral' nomads following their livestock from summer to winter grazing areas. Today the Bedouin men in the south Sinai mostly move between their family homes and the tourist areas.

...the desert, as a site conceived as a place on to which to project one's other self which is in need of spiritual re-awakening, takes on a quite different political resonance when it, along with its associated metaphors of the tent and the nomad, is constructed as the space inhabited by 'others' whose sole function is the reinvigoration of the jaded Western self (2003: 132).

While Orientalist-influenced films, brochures and marketing establish these links, it is the gendered and racialised objectification of the (Arab) Bedouin man that contributes to the construction of the desert as temporarily stalled, a place 'out of time' that can be experienced most directly through the body in a sexual/romantic encounter in the safety of tourist space.

In the Sinai, local men are considered desirable, not just because they are attractive and available, but because of certain assumptions about their imagined masculinity. Although these masculinities can vary when described – they are more close to Nature, more 'manly', or 'real gentlemen' – they are not only put in a comparative position to a nominal notion of Western masculinity (which is presented as undesirable) they are inextricably entwined with the positioning of these men within their historicized landscape. Without the landscape, the masculinity (as it is described by the women) falters.

Petra, 19 and her friend Lena, 21, were student nurses from Switzerland on their first holiday to Sharm El Sheikh. Both had found young Egyptian boyfriends from among their hotel staff within the first two days of their arrival. They told me that unlike the Swiss men they knew, Egyptian men were charming, polite and solicitous – they were 'real gentlemen'. Sabine, 27, also from Switzerland, was a nanny for a Swiss family on her second visit to Sharm El Sheikh, who was causing great confusion at her hotel by choosing a different man from the staff to go out with each night. She also described her dates (most of whom she slept with) as 'gentlemen' who, in turn, treated her like a 'lady'.

American photographer (and Sinai image maker) Karen had made her base approximately 100km away in the Bedouin/backpacker village in Dahab (Asilah). It is Karen who called the Sinai 'an approachable wilderness'. Yet in order to maintain this image of wilderness she needed the Bedouin male inhabitants to continue to wear their traditional nomadic attire of white *galabeyas*. She complained to me of the difficulties posed by Bedouins who preferred to wear 'modern' clothes like jeans and baseball caps. This was not the image that sold pictures. In addition their change of clothing contributed to spoiling their purity and disrupted their symbolic connection to the landscape. For her, this change was not welcome:

> ...they [the Bedouin] were so pure in their thinking, so naïve, like children, not knowing that something would harm them. At the same time a bit hostile, a bit violent because that was in their nature (Karen, 40, Dahab, September 2000).

This sentiment echoes the comments of Victorian traveller Mary Kingsley that the natives she met in Africa were child-like, which as Mills points out was a 'standard colonial statement' (1998: 92). For women today it could also mean that the attractiveness of local men's masculinity – an Orientalist masculinity so closely associated with Nature but also with violence and inferiority – is seriously compromised if they switch to Levis.[3]

Karen's expression of regret would also seem to be a straightforward statement of nostalgia for a Sinai she thought was passing. However it isn't the expression of longing for a Sinai from the colonial period or a premodern Sinai as such, but for a Sinai that could *still* be experienced as premodern. The Sinai she misses is the Sinai she first visited it in the late 1980s, a Sinai in hiatus between its previous occupation by Israel and its soon to be occupation and development by Egypt. Many women like Karen have been visiting the Sinai for over 15 years and for them the development of a local 'modernity' was a recent and unwelcome development they had personally witnessed, yet never implicated themselves in.

For the last two years, Susanne, a Swiss woman in her late sixties and grandmother of three, had been dividing her time between her biologist husband in Zurich and her Egyptian lover Adel – a manager of a small hotel in the Tarrabin area of Nuweiba. When I met her she was in the process of buying an apartment for herself and Adel, with her husband's knowledge. She told me why she found men from the Sinai so attractive:

> I tell you...you can put me (in front of) one hundred naked Caribbean men, nothing with me. A nice body. And here you can put one man in a *galabeya* and everything in my face change. Not a naked man. They (Bedouin men) are one with Nature and most of them are one with God (Susanne, 67, Nuweiba, 2000).

As I have mentioned in the preface, for the Western female, ethnosexual encounters are still very much defined by, and associated with, Western white women and black African-Caribbean men who meet in the tourist resorts of the Caribbean. However, while men might accept the label of 'sex tourist' most of the women I interviewed certainly did not see themselves as sex tourists and their relationships were often presented as incidental or even accidental to their holiday, rather than as the sole or primary motive. And, as we have seen, when they did compare their sexual relationships, they tended to compare them to their relationships with men in (and from) their own country. Susanne was the only woman I interviewed who made a direct comparison between her sexual relationship with a younger Egyptian man and sexual tourism in the Caribbean. This shift of focus can also be seen in Susanne's comments about the Bedouin. Like Karen and other women I spoke to, his 'traditional' galabeya indicates he is connected to Nature. In the Western

---

3   Some Egyptian interviewees admitted to dressing in what they considered to be a Bedouin style (mostly wearing a keffiyeh) to emphasise their 'localness' because they believed it made them more attractive to women visitors.

imagination, this form of clothing is also synonymous with Biblical imagery and for Susanne it represented the Bedouin's connection with religion and 'God'. However Susanne focuses more on the men's racial and sexual construction – in particular on their bodies: by directly comparing them to Caribbean men. They are not only naked, they are many and indistinguishable. They are placed in front of *her* – she gives herself the position of sovereign subject, the one who chooses. A sexual relationship with a Bedouin man doesn't just offer her sex (as inferred by her reference to men in the Caribbean), but a spiritual connection to Nature.

Here, one racialised and sexualised stereotype of masculinity in the Third World is being rejected in favour of another; a valorised Orientalist version that has been co-opted to legitimise a sexual relationship with a younger and less privileged man. Although Susanne told me she likes to visits poor areas in Cairo where she dispenses money and gifts to families who live there, any cultural and economic disparity between herself and her Egyptian lover is ignored. Her relationship perhaps involved the largest age gap but by inscribing her relationship with spiritual values in the context of the Caribbean alternative, she has elevated her ethnosexual tourism to a more worthy purpose.

Despite women's valorisation of, and attraction to this sexually constructed idea of Bedouin masculinity, actual relationships with Bedouin men often fell short of such imaginings. Although Susanne chose to spend her days in a Bedouin (tourist) village, she was actually in a relationship with an Egyptian man, not a Bedouin. For many women Bedouin men were considered to be difficult to sustain longer-term relationships with. In the end, location was more important. Marianne, a former special needs teacher from Germany, told me about a series of relationships she had had in the Sinai over the years – with Bedouins, Egyptians and a Sudanese man. What mattered and what made them 'real men' was not where they came from as much as where they were based (although she and many others never became involved with Western residents). For Marianne (and others) what mattered was her sense of their belonging to the Sinai landscape (in her case this meant the Bedouin-style tourist beach camps of Nuweiba).

> I mean they are real man... (in the Sinai). They know how things are going. They know what they want or what they...the way they are. It's more clear, they are more clear. In Germany everything is more in between, so it's also more easy to be a woman, when you are with a man in the Sinai...When I start to come here, my interest in German men stopped, khallas [finished] (Marianne, 39, Tarrabin, Nuweiba, September 2000).

When Marianne compares men in the Sinai to men in Germany, she is clearly expressing an ethnicised preference. She finds the men she meets in the Sinai more attractive because her idea of local Bedouin/Arab masculinity is one that is more distinct from femininity than found between men and women in Europe. In response Marianne felt free to perform a version of femininity she felt unable to perform in Europe:

> I mean, don't misunderstand me. I don't want to say I'm just a woman and I'm
> not...I like this feeling. I like (it) if the man is very clear and you can fight it
> and you can show (it), also you express yourself more (Marianne, 39, Tarrabin,
> Nuweiba, September 2000).

By being with a real man, she can be a real woman, freed from the feeling of
confusion surrounding her gendered identity in Europe, at least while she remained
outside.

Steffanie, who we met in Chapter 3, came to Egypt when she was 21, on her
first solo trip away from her native Switzerland. A practising Christian at the time,
she told me her trip was inspired by a Biblical imagination of Moses receiving the
Ten Commandments on Mount Sinai. While she also felt that 'men were more male'
Steffanie was also attracted to what she considered to be a spiritual atmosphere in the
Sinai where 'everyone you meet is talking about religion'. She was staying in a hotel
in Cairo popular with backpackers when she first heard about the Bedouin tourist
village in Dahab. She visited and met and Eqyptian man there on her first day. He was
in his forties and already married with children but by the end of her first week she
had married him and converted to Islam. Her interpretation of the (ancient Biblical)
landscape *and* the local masculinity not only allowed her to change her religious
identity; it also gave her the opportunity to experience a different (historicised)
version of herself through her perception of gendered identity.

> I feel men (in Sinai) are romantic and they can give a woman a lot. Because they
> are... more male...more men. With their pride and how to behave in this society.
> As a woman they give you the feeling they are strong. I feel that I'm available as
> a woman...I feel here that just being a woman is already...enough...I visit this
> man, I want him. I fell in love with him (Steffanie, 26, Dahab, April 2000).

The modern travelling subject is conceptualised as male and sovereign over a
feminised and conquered landscape. He wanders at will – he certainly doesn't
use charter flights or pack sun tan lotion. Yet, as Pasztory notes, civilisation (of
which modernity is one form) is also constructed as a kind of feminine nostalgia,
'searching for that lost, masculine lover' (2001: 18).

Landscape, in the seductive combination of a space that is simultaneously seen
to exist outside of modernity yet be an accessible tourist space, is crucial to these
relationships. A common assumption about men like Steffanie's husband is that they
marry foreign women in order to obtain a passport to Europe or North America
(Yuval-Davis 1997). Yet, in their nostalgic search for Pasztory's lost masculine
lover, it would seem that women who travel to the Sinai today don't always want to
follow the nineteenth century tradition of 'civilising' native men by bringing them
to Europe or North America. As Western modernity continues its spread across once
remote landscapes, it is now more common that, as Pasztory suggests, 'princesses
are no longer taking the peasant to their palaces; instead they are forsaking their
courts to move into thatched huts with their native heroes' (2001: 19).

The men they encounter might still want to go to Europe or North America, as did the Egyptian husbands of two women interviewees who subsequently moved on to Europe and the United States. But in both these cases their wives remained in the Sinai. And Steffanie, after getting married, also stayed. She opened a small, basic hotel, established with her capital, contacts and IT skills and her husband's local connections. Still in her early thirties, she now has two three star hotels and continues to upgrade her accommodation. Her ethnosexual encounter and subsequent marriage based upon a gendered, romantic, religious geographical imagination of a place and people 'out of time' gave her access to a new identity and a business opportunity where she can reproduce this imagination of place for other visitors from Europe.

Honorary Men and the Ethnomasquerade

As we can see, the landscape of the Sinai is relatively varied in terms of its appeal to visitors and while many women head straight for the beach resorts of Sharm El Sheikh, a not insignificant number preferred the Bedouin tourist village of Dahab and the Bedouin beach camps that are dotted around Nuweiba. For these women the attraction was more the lifestyle of the Bedouin and what Pasztory (2001) calls 'nostalgia for mud' which she defines as, 'ascribing higher spiritual values to people and cultures considered lower than oneself, the romanticisation of the faraway primitive (2001: 17).[4]

According to Birkett (1989) Victorian women travellers were not different from men in their tendency to construct the people they encountered as belonging to a 'primitive culture'. However, they were more likely than men to express a positive account of this culture and express a desire to prevent it from being irreparably changed by the modernising forces of progress:

> Neither the construction of an ancient and primitive culture, nor the self-awareness of this creation, was peculiar to women travellers, but was shared by both male and female intruders into exotic societies throughout the nineteenth and earlier twentieth centuries. The quest for the lost self in the sands of the desert, the undergrowth of the jungle, the inland waterways of a tropical swamp, was a common motif in their accounts... How female eyes did differ, however, was in the development of this myth of a primitive society and the uses to which they put it. Women saw, confronted and then put enormous energy into trying to prevent any further intrusion on their outdated visions by European influence, an effort which threw them against the combined and eventually insurmountable

---

4   The author Martin Amis also uses this term – in its original French – *Nostalgia de la Boue* – which he defines as 'a childish, even babyish delight in bodily functions and wastes' in an article on Pornography in the *Saturday Guardian* ('A Rough Trade' pp. 8–14, 17 March 2001).

forces of expanding colonisation, cultural assimilation, proselytization and the demands and ambitions of the exotic peoples themselves (1989: 147).

If anything, postcolonial travel has not dented these binaried constructions of 'primitive culture' but continues to reinforce them. For Beezer (1993), Third World adventure travel is a movement between two worlds: the Western world which is the cause of the traveller's problems, and the world of travel, which is a kind of patchwork, 'a series of places, an infinite number of locales to be 'discovered'' (1993: 123).⁵ The ethnic encounter (as marketed in adventure travel literature) is sold as a cure for the malaise of the Western would-be traveller – the encounter is expected to provide physical and spiritual nourishment. Tomlinson (1991) argues that the contemplation of other cultures is an 'exportation of loss' which allows us the sense of escape from the contradictions inherent in the condition of modernity.

> It is as though the Third World is attributed with a special need and even a special *responsibility* to resist the enticements of an ersatz commodified culture. They have mint tea and the 'natural' cultural practices of breast-feeding; they are somehow, closer to the 'basic needs' that we have lost with affluence. Therefore we should look to their 'innocence' as the hope of our own cultural salvation – *this* is why they need 'protection' (1991: 120).

While the anti-modern woman tourist associates both the landscape and Bedouin people with the spiritual values of Nature and God, the position of the Egyptian man is more ambivalent. Being neither 'native' nor Westerner, being both modern and pre/un/anti-modern, Egyptian men tend to sit uneasily in this geographical imagination.

As I mentioned previously, Victorian women travellers such as Isabelle Eberhardt and Gertrude Bell discovered the advantages of going 'native' by adopting local dress and customs (often disguising themselves as men) and becoming 'Queens of the Desert'. The anti-modern women tourist as native first appeared in the Sinai in the 1970s, when European and Israeli women visiting the Sinai encountered Bedouin men. Since then a small but not insignificant number of women have not only met (and married into) Bedouin communities but also adopted the dress and customs of Bedouin life; mostly young women from the smaller provincial cities and towns of northern Europe.

Nora, who was mentioned in Chapter 3, was a 22-year-old trainee nurse in Switzerland when she first came to the Sinai in the early 1990s on a two-week holiday with a group of friends. She met Ahmed, a Bedouin on the beach in Nuweiba. It was 'love at first sight' and she returned a few months later to marry and settle with him in his desert home. At first she lived with his family in the

---

5   Beezer argues that it is often women and nature, condensed into a single figure, which are made into representatives of the 'otherness' the Western traveller seeks'. This study, of course, deals with women as Western travellers.

mountains away from the tourist coast and was taught the Bedouin Arabic dialect and customs by Ahmed's mother and sisters. She told me that she started out in jeans and t-shirts but gradually she stopped dressing as a European and adopted the clothes of a Bedouin woman. After about six months the couple moved to a small hut made of palm tree fronds on a relatively isolated stretch of the coast near Nuweiba where she lives today. When I interviewed her in 2000 this hut was her main home. She lived there with her three young sons without electricity and cooked on an open fire. Her husband was away working as a guide for tourists many of whom were friends, or friends of friends from Switzerland.

Nora didn't just fall in love with Ahmed, but with the whole way of life. Moving in with his family gave her what she felt was unique access to the people and landscape and to understanding it.

> When you live…you have to live it to understand. You can't be without to live
> it to understand….When I come here I was living in the village. It was difficult,
> very difficult. It's not for everybody. It's not for everybody at all. But when you
> go through, I go through because I want to live it and I want to understand…
> (Nora, 34, Nuweiba, April 2000).

For Nora and others who have taken on similar positions in Bedouin society, the difficulties and hardships they encounter and endure seem to be a major part of the attraction and proof of the authenticity of their experience. Modernity might be stressful and complex and Bedouin life simple and pure, but Nora is also proud of her ability to forego the comforts of modernity. Being accepted by her host family, accepted in a way Nora feels most tourists and foreigners are not, is of major importance. She sees her life with the Bedouin women as a form of education, not that dissimilar to the ethnographer/anthropologist. And unlike the tourist 'outsider', the rewards were unrivalled insider access to a primitive and premodern and unmodern life. An access obtained through her relationship with Ahmed.

> …after all the big school I get much back. So much. I can't tell you. Now I'm
> really in the family. I'm not outside anymore. Before I was outside. It's like this.
> If you don't live it you can't understand. You can't be inside, not possible, no
> way (Nora, 34, Nuweiba, April 2000).

While Nora was living as a modern European she was implicated in the modernity. Now she has discovered the effect of the ethnomasquerade and become a Bedouin she can be 'inside', she is 'out' of Europe and has entered 'in' to another place.

> I'm very glad I'm out of it, of the system what we…how I was living. I live in
> another kind of system, but it's not so tight. It's less tight (Nora, 34, Nuweiba,
> April 2000).

Pasztory argues that a rejection of civilisation by primitivists such as Nora does not mean a rejection of technology.

> We believe in technology, regardless of what we say to the contrary, and we believe that archaic or low class persons have developed technologies of the spirit that we envy or wish to acquire (2001: 18).

While Nora might envy the technologies of the spirit that she believes can be found in a pure form of Bedouin life (in the mountains away from the tourist coast) Nora has not completely renounced her origins and accompanying privileges. She travels once a year to visit her family in Switzerland and holds onto her and her sons' Swiss passports. Escaping modernity however is not that easy and its desirability is ambiguous. For the problem with travelling, whether it is with a backpack or a suitcase, is that your destinations inevitably become sullied by your presence. Antimodern women like Nora often believe their positionality is the same as the Bedouins. However while antimodern women look upon the large-scale tourist developments in Sinai as eyesores and view the 'modern' infrastructure introduced by the Egyptian government for Bedouin communities with horror, the Bedouin often have a more ambivalent attitude. While they might resent the Egyptian concrete housing, schools and hospitals they are provided with, it usually isn't on aesthetic grounds. Rather, Bedouins are keenly aware that, when it comes to state resources, they come second to the families of the newly-arrived migrant Egyptians.

'Thatched huts' might be desirable because they are crucial to the successful imaginings of 'out of time' place. However, they work because they are within tourist resorts like those found in the Sinai, so can provide women with a position of privilege, and an almost sovereign subjectivity of safety. Women are able to 'lose themselves' yet stay in control because of their access to greater economic and cultural capital because of their status as honorary men. Women – who often spoke of how they felt unimportant in their own society – discovered that in the Sinai they were treated like royalty. As Susanne told me about her life in Egypt:

> ...yes, I feel me like a queen (Susanne, 67, Nuweiba 2000).

Conclusion

In their research, Pruitt and LaFont noted the apparent contradiction among women tourists in the Caribbean, who adopt nominally 'masculine' behaviour – such as initiating relationships and being the partner with the main source of income – yet at the same time are attracted to what they call 'conventional' ideas of masculinity. They note how, 'ideas about masculine power are central to the women's attraction to local men' (1995: 436).

Nominally conservative ideas of masculinity and power also circulate around Western women's ethnosexual encounters with 'local' men in the Sinai. Women are often the major wage-earner and, in general, have a greater access to economic and cultural capital than their partner. The men are often chosen by the women and might also be significantly younger than them.

Yet, they say the men appeal to them because of their essentialised and geographically specific masculinity. These women can also be said to have adopted another version of a dominant masculinity – the positionality of the modern (male) travelling subject. They tend to travel independently from their families, occupy a significant position in (male) public space and assume the positionality of the honorary man.

Pruitt and LaFont conclude that the 'masculine' behaviour exhibited by the women they met in the Caribbean meant that they were effectively testing 'the constraints of conventional gender identity present in western culture' (1995: 435). In the twenty-first century, nominally masculine behaviour such as initiating relationships and being the partner with the higher income cannot be said to be unique to ethnosexual tourist-local relationships. The difference lies then, not in the women's sexual behaviour between their own and their host country, but its purpose – to experience a more satisfying ideal of femininity through the adoption of a 'masculine' identity. This is not so much a challenge to perceived gendered and racial inequalities, as an escape from them through imagined, emotional (time) travel.

The Sinai – emotionally imagined and experienced as a Biblical/Victorian paradise-desert – is crucial to the imagined and experienced masculinity within these relationships; the imagined masculinity of local men is key to imagining and experiencing an out of time paradise-desert. These 'othered' masculinities combine with paradise-desert touristscapes to produce a powerful and emotive imaginative geography of gendered colonial nostalgia.

The ambivalence tourist women felt towards local gender relations varied, but were, perhaps unsurprisingly, rarely articulated. In interviews they rarely questioned the relative absence of Egyptian/Bedouin women in their day-to-day lives, or their position in relation to these women. Their 'husbands' often had Egyptian wives (and children) elsewhere in the country, but this seemed an acceptable part of the relationship.[6]

As emancipatory as Pruitt and LaFont's testing of gender constraints might sound, the same testing can also be viewed with alarm in the host society. At the same time as these men are being desired for their alleged masculinity, their involvement with Western women is also seen as part of a process of their feminisation. Ebron has commented on the negative state reaction to female 'sex tourism' in Gambia:

---

6 Marriage was also surprisingly acceptable. Because it is illegal for unmarried couples in Egypt to live together, legal contracts of marriage (paper or *orfi* marriages) are used and often entered into very lightly. One 27-year-old diving instructor I interviewed in Dahab had gone through 14 of these contracts.

> When powerful Northern women are thought to be stalking junior Southern
> men, a disturbing gender inversion has occurred. Gambian men are feminized.
> National honor and masculinity are jeopardized (1997: 227).

In Egypt the response has been similar – if the man is from a lower socio-economic
background. For example, while it is illegal for unmarried couples to book a hotel
room, middle class Egyptian men (or male tourists from the Gulf) are rarely
questioned. Yet in the cheaper parts of Dahab and Nuweiba, where the Egyptian
men are less economically advantaged, this rule is enforced with vigour through
the tourist police. This discrepancy, suggests Behbehanian (2000), is down to the
fact that when the rich(er) tourist is female, the 'result is a disturbing emasculation
which strikes a national chord' (2000: 34).

   Calling ethnosexual tourist-local encounters 'romance tourism' (Pruitt and
LaFont) leaves research prone to accusations of essentialism if 'romance' is only
applied to the women's attitude to their relationships with men from Third World
tourist destinations. Romance *is* crucial to these relationships but it is the romance
of a nostalgic engagement with the past through the historicised objectification of
native masculinities *and* (a highly selective part of) their living environment.

   These relationships might well depend on the concept of 'fixity' in the
ideological construction of otherness as Bhabha notes of colonialism. In the
Western imagination of Arab Bedouins it might seem contradictory then, that they
are constantly on the move. However, they are never allowed to arrive anywhere.
Bedouins in Sinai are perceived as a tourist attraction (and are therefore attractive
to tourists) because they conjure up a nostalgic search for authenticity that remains
one of what MacCannell (1999) calls the 'components of the conquering spirit of
modernity'. The desert, supposedly inhabited by seductively masculine nomads
in a pure natural state, ostensibly in perpetual motion, yet who are inevitably
fixed by both a temporal construction of otherness and Fabian's related 'denial
of coevalness' (1983) they somehow exist outside our modernity. Tourist space
in the Sinai is consumed by the modern subject as an alternative to modernity, an
absence of modernity and a pre-modernity.

   Without the promise of an intimate and personal encounter with a desert-
paradise landscape these men would soon lose their appeal. Without these men,
and their historicised masculinity, the desert would really be 'empty' – a feminised,
impoverished landscape, with limited access, stripped of its ability to take these
women to another place and time.

Chapter 5
Re-imagined Masculinities – From Marginal to Hyperreal

Introduction

The Orient, is according to Said, 'almost a European invention', and an invention that 'since antiquity' has been loaded with sexual, and sensual meaning, portrayed as 'a place of romance, exotic beings, haunting memories and landscapes and remarkable experiences' (1978: 1) Although I have chosen mainly to focus on the imaginations and positionalities of Western women tourists, in this chapter I will examine some of the issues that have been raised in previous chapters as they apply to the men who become involved in sexual and romantic relationships with women tourists in the Sinai.

To date I have concentrated on Western women tourists and argued that they travel to the Sinai in order to escape from Western modernity and that their ethnosexual encounters with local Egyptian and Bedouin men are based upon seeing the landscape and men of the Sinai as representative of some alternative to, or absence of, modernity. Other studies on women engaging in sexual tourism in the Third World have, like me, tended to focus on the women, with relatively little attention given to the men in these relationships. When the focus does shift, it is usually argued that these men engage in sexual encounters with Western women primarily for sexual and/or economic motives.

Yuval-Davis, for example, suggests that having sex with foreign women appeals because, quite simply, 'local men get free sex' in cultures where local women are kept 'under strict social control,' (1997: 52). Bowman (1996) concurs, suggesting that in the Old City of Jerusalem local men's sexual frustration is a major factor in the men's decision to pursue tourist women, and comes from living in a society where sex outside marriage is frowned upon.

Economic factors also matter, not just concerning the Third World status of the tourist destination, but also in connection with the economic status of many of the men involved in these relationships. Phillips points out the 'low socioeconomic background' of the beach hustler (1999: 186) in her ethnographic study of what she terms 'male tourist-oriented prostitution' in Barbados, while Sanchez Taylor's (2001) survey of foreign women 'sex tourists' in the Dominican Republic and Jamaica also notes that most of the boys and men involved in this activity are working class. She argues that, even if the women themselves are reluctant to admit it,

> …most beach boys enter into sexual relationships with as many tourist women
> as they possibly can, and most of these relationships result in some form of
> material or economic benefit for the man (2001: 757).

In their study on Kuta Cowboys in Bali, Dahles and Bras (1999) argue that the young men who frequent Kuta beach in the resort town of Bali, Indonesia are 'romantic entrepreneurs' – choosing to highlight the resourcefulness of the young men who are effectively creating an opportunity to earn an income where none previously existed. Other studies have suggested that the ultimate aim of these relationships is marriage, a First World passport and emigration to the West. Cohen, for example, concludes that 'Arab' boys in Akka, Israel, have romances with foreign girls in order to escape their economic situation and move to Europe or North America.

   Most of these explanations tend to tie in with perspectives of the Third World that highlight a process of feminisation by the First. Offering sex for money highlights your lack of power, and your lack of alternative means to obtain economic resources other than to sell your own body. However, in his study of Palestinian shopkeepers, Bowman proposes that far from passively catering to the sexual needs of Western women, the sexual behaviour of men in Jerusalem's Old City is aggressive, a response to feelings of emasculation rather than part of the process of feminisation. He describes these sexual relationships as a reassertion of masculinity (almost hypermasculinity) with sex for 'conquest' fuelled by a desire for 'revenge'. Moreover the women are not the primary targets of this revenge; rather it is the Western men who, it is assumed, are the proprietors of these women. In this highly masculinist fantasy the women themselves are almost insignificant, merely acting as channels for their frustration.

> Their relative powerlessness in the face of the vacillating demands of groups of
> foreigners endowed with economic and social superiority was counterbalanced,
> in the particular setting of the Jerusalem *suq* (market), by the development of an
> aggressive sexuality focused on the women of the tourist populations (1996: 87).

The financial opportunities afforded by initiating relationships with European women certainly contribute towards their proliferation in the Sinai. But while there is strong evidence that the relative inequity in the economic situation between local men and European and North American women can be a crucial factor in these relationships, it does not explain all the relationships that occur or really give us enough information about their content and acknowledge their complexity. Relationships between local men and foreign women in the Sinai are not always distinguished by an extreme difference in income or wealth, particularly when the woman involved was under 30. And, while ethnosexual tourist-local encounters in Bali, West Africa and the Caribbean might be predominantly with men from low socio-economic backgrounds, in the Sinai, a not insignificant number of men were comfortably middle class and well educated, sometimes far more so than their girlfriends.

What was noticeable, however, was that these men still spoke of feeling 'second class' in relation to Europeans and North Americans and saw a Western girlfriend and/or wife as a means to acquire and access this cultural capital – a form of capital that their economic wealth alone could not give them. An Egyptian lawyer, Hamdi, tried to explain the attraction of Western women to me by comparing them to the many Russian women who are now visiting the region and also engaging in relationships with local men. He told me that these women, who are often indistinguishable from their European counterparts at a distance, (except perhaps that they dress more glamorously) were like 'a rose without a scent.'

Whether it was the woman's youth or her (relative) wealth, it was clear that by establishing a successful relationship with a foreign woman, a local man's options were greatly improved. These relationships offered the men power in the personal sphere and elsewhere that might be lacking in other parts of their lives. A power that was not merely financial, but strongly linked to increased social mobility. Access to this power was facilitated by the woman's secondary gendered status, particularly in the way it could be controlled through the institution of marriage and/or rules of foreign business partnerships under Egyptian state law.

While a passport to another life in Europe or North America was definitely a target for some men, only those from the lowest socio-economic backgrounds wanted to move permanently. For many men with a degree of education and strong family links, the aim was rather to be able to access the mobility of the Western citizen (and the positionality of the modern male subject) and also establish business opportunities in the Sinai. If these relationships were an escape from modernity for many women; for the men they offered an escape *to* modernity. However it was by no means necessary to leave Egypt in order to achieve this aim.

The men in these relationships have also been influenced by the dominating geographical imagination that places them at the margins, on the periphery of modernity and Europe and the West in the centre. Just as it has been argued that the behaviour and appearance of women in the Middle East are seen to represent cultural values (Moghadam 1993, Kandyoti 1991), women in the West are very much seen not only to offer, but also embody Western values and modernity. And, just as the women seek encounters and create relationships with local men as a 'way in' to another existence, many men see a relationship with a foreign woman as a 'way in' to modernity.

The ambivalence offered by the women's gendered status meant that engaging in relationships and marriage with these women could therefore offer men an alternative form of interaction with modernity, and one that was far less confrontational and purely exploitative than those offered by global neoliberalism.

This goes some of the way to explain why men do not necessarily need or want to move to Europe or North America. There is growing awareness among many men that their relationship with the West would be far harder to sustain to their advantage if they leave the relative safety of Sinai tourist space and move to a dominant Western society, where their non-white masculinity is more marginalised than pedestalised. In addition there is a genuine love of their home, both in Egypt and the Sinai, and a dislike of colder climates that is not just metaphorical. Many Egyptian and Bedouin men may want access to modernity, but they want it on their terms, in their own home, not as a stranger in a strange land. And, if they did want to move away permanently, they would sometimes meet resistance from their partners, who, as we have seen, often got involved with a man linked to the Sinai just so they could escape from their own country in the first place. Ellen, 44, from the United States, for example, fell in love with Egypt while a student on her travels and married an Egyptian man she met who worked at the American Embassy in Cairo. They are now divorced and he lives in America while she has remarried and lives in Sharm El Sheikh.

In this way, many relationships are confined to the tourist resorts of the Sinai where they began, and where modernity is seen to coexist, albeit in tension, with imaginations of an unmodern, premodern and antimodern Sinai. Tensions that perhaps are created by the different way in which the resorts of the Sinai are perceived; Sharm El Sheikh for example might be an exotic Oriental resort to visiting tourist women from Western Europe and North America, but to Egyptian men it is often referred to as the 'California of Egypt', a space of ultramodernity. Yet it is this very ambiguity surrounding the tourist spaces of the Sinai that allow local men and foreign women to believe they have both achieved their aim, to escape from and to modernity.

The Occidental Tourist

In many ways Egyptian and Bedouin men's attitudes towards the West can be said to be expressed in terms of an Occidental geographical imagination. Although I am suitably aware of the effect of unhelpful dichotomies, by referencing its (supposed) opposite – Orientalism – Occidentalism can help describe these imaginations of both self and other presented here as a part of the process of Orientalism discussed in previous chapters. This is not another binary of opposition because Occidentalism is not just a simple reaction to the stereotypical construction of the Middle East and its population for the purposes of domination. Occidentalism is situated *within* Orientalism in that it internalises and to a large degree accepts Orientalist notions of self and other, in a similar way to Pratt's (1992) use of 'autoethnography' to 'refer to instances in which colonized subjects undertake to represent themselves in ways that *engage with* the colonizer's own terms' and involve 'partial collaboration with and appropriation of the idioms of the conqueror' (1992: 7). Like stereotypes in general, Occidentalism is reductionist and simplistic but speaks of different issues of power relations – Orientalist stereotypes of gender and race and their maintenance of inequalities of power.

The Bedouin and Egyptian men working in tourism that I interviewed in the Sinai, expressed a wide range of attitudes towards Europe (and the West in general) that were heavily influenced by their perception of their own and their country's relative power, economic development, culture and wealth.

In general, North America and Western Europe (and their citizenry) were seen as very modern when compared to life in Egypt, but this modernity was often described by the men in undesirable terms: such as 'too fast', 'too hectic', 'too obsessed with work', and a favourite phrase 'too cold'. Khaled, 28, worked as chief animation at a resort hotel in Sharm El Sheikh. He was responsible for a large team of young Italian and Egyptians whose job it was to ensure the guests enjoyed their stay in the hotel. His response to the supposed superiority of a European masculinity was common among the men I interviewed:

> Sure. European men are cold people, in the sense of not feeling. You compare them to the Latin blood or the Egyptian people. European people are rich, Middle East is poor in a way, poor means you know what it is to live hard, so you are very sensitive in a way because you suffer to live... OK you do not have money. You go to Europe you can never find this... (Khaled, 28, Sharm El Sheikh, August 2000).

In this way, according to Khaled and many other men in the Sinai, what they lacked in money was more than made up for by the possession of a superior form of masculinity expressed in sexual terms. This could be their sensitivity, their passion or even their sexual stamina, but the masculinity of their Western counterparts was always viewed as somehow lacking and the proof offered was the way in which so many women came from Europe and North America to seek them out for sexual relationships. Eid was a 29-year-old Bedouin who, though he was originally from the mountainous region of Sinai, now worked as a divemaster and safari guide in the backpacker/Bedouin tourist resort of Dahab. Eid was fully aware of the degree to which his mobility was severely restricted, especially when he compared himself to the ever-mobile tourists. He had never been to Europe, and, perhaps as a result of his restricted mobility, the Europe he imagined was not one he wanted to visit. He told me he didn't want to go to a place that Europeans couldn't wait to get away from themselves.

> ...people run from something, from tiring, from working (Eid, 28, Dahab, September 2000).

Jamal, 25, was also a Bedouin and worked as a receptionist at a small hotel in Sharm El Sheikh run by a Bedouin family. He was relatively new to the resort, and had come from the town of El-Tur, a Bedouin community and Egyptian administrative centre 90km north of Sharm El Sheikh. So far he had had relatively few tourist girlfriends. He had never been to Europe, but had already decided what it was like from his conversations with tourists:

You know it's not easy to work there, it's not easy to live there (in Europe). Here
I work eight hours, but it's not like in Europe. In Europe it's working, that mean
what? Work is work, nothing else. Here it's easier. Everything goes slowly and
it's easier (Jamal, 25, Sharm El Sheikh, April 2000).

The link between the cold climate and hard working conditions and a lack of
sex (and sexuality) was often made, by men who had never been to Europe
or North America, and by those who had gone and subsequently returned. In
contrast of course, the amount of free time available to tourists and the warm
sultry climate of the Sinai had the opposite effect. Ali, 36, was part Egyptian,
part Berber and worked as a diving instructor in Dahab. He had been married
twice before, once to a woman from Ireland and once to a Dutch woman. He has
also lived for several years in the Netherlands. At the time of the interview he
was involved with an American woman, a fellow diver who shared an apartment
with him in Dahab. He told me that European women soon lost their inhibitions
about indulging in sexual relationships with uneducated local men in the Sinai
because of a combination of factors: an unprecedented amount of male attention,
the seductive qualities of a warm climate, and the general paradise landscape
that Sinai offered:

　　Let's put it that way. Come on, in England, or in Europe – it's cold, it's miserable.
　　And then you come here and you go out and you have a lovely time. With a nice
　　guy. Yeah, he's from the Middle East, he's not well educated, he's not open
　　minded, but he's nice. The reflect(ion) of the moonlight on his face is nice. And
　　then this thing it come up... (Ali, 36, Dahab, October 2000).

Ultra-modern, Hyperreal Sinai

In previous chapters I discussed how Egypt is imagined and experienced as an
exotic ancient and traditional Oriental environment by women tourists. In general
this imagination is not shared by the men – except perhaps in reference to St.
Catherine's Monastery and Mount Sinai and occasionally in reference to the
Bedouin communities (by Egyptian men). From a local perspective of course the
history of Egypt is seen as proof of a rich cultural heritage rather than evidence
of an unbroken link to a condition of premodernity or unmodernity. If anything,
Sinai and especially Sharm El Sheikh, with its huge tourist resorts and Western
bars, restaurants and clubs, as mentioned earlier, was seen as 'ultra-modern' and
the 'California' of Egypt.

　　Aside from Egypt's nationalist projects of modernity such as the Aswan dam
and the latter day Suez Canal, the tourist industry infrastructure is perhaps the
central, certainly the most visually dominant, aspect of Egypt's engagement with
modernity. The infrastructure of airports, roads, resorts and luxury villas and

apartments also act as the primary zones of encounter with Western modernity, through the millions of tourists that visit Egypt every year.[1]

But while the Sinai is a space of modernity for many of the Egyptian men I interviewed, its inhabitants – the Bedouin – were often imagined as unmodern and premodern. Although this viewpoint was very similar to that of Western women; unlike Western women, opinion was divided as to whether their presence was desirable or not. For the men who expressed a pride in the modernity of the Sinai resorts the 'traditional' Bedouin were sometimes viewed as embarrassing and unwelcome and their way of life seen as 'uncivilised'. Other Egyptian men, however, found Bedouin culture, particularly its myths of a hyperreal masculinity appealing and made great efforts to be accepted among the local Bedouin community. In a localised version of the ethnomasquerade they were also fully aware of the romantic opportunities offered by a well-placed *keffiyeh* when they navigated their tourist encounters with Western women.

At the time of my interview with him, Amr was 28, a wealthy, young Egyptian man from the Nile Delta who ran a business renting motorbikes for desert excursions in Sharm El Sheikh. Amr, and his young male Egyptian staff, often wore *keffiyehs* (with jeans) and were happy to be mistaken for Bedouins by visiting tourists as it helped to authenticate their desert trips and (as they told me) made them more attractive. He admired the Bedouin men he met there, and saw them and their lifestyle as the epitome of cool:

> I do like these people. I do really like. They keep their word. They really keep their word. They have principles, they have morals, they have their own life, no matter if they are very, very rich or they don't have nothing, It's still the same. Living the same way. They won't change (Amr, 28, Sharm El Sheikh, May 2000).

Amr and other Egyptian men like him are also examples of how Orientalism needs to be viewed as a complex and ambivalent process. On the one hand these men wanted to be admired and wished to benefit from a reflected image of Bedouin masculinity, but on the other they were outsiders who (like many women from Europe) felt emotional and historical ties to the desert landscape. Amr told me how he couldn't wait to visit after the Sinai became part of Egypt in 1982 and how he 'fell in love' with the desert after a visit to the Bedouin village of Dahab (and first started a business there renting jetskis). And like many women from Europe, his business ventures (often with European women partners) were often a means to allow him to live in the Sinai.

---

1 The Suez Canal, Suez tunnel, Aswan dam and the new industrial cities outside Cairo are also major emblems of modernity in Egypt but are rarely on Western visitors tourist itineraries.

Figure 5.1   Egyptian staff of a beachfront watersports centre with friends in Na'ama Bay, Sharm El Sheikh

Source: Jessica Jacobs (2001).

Marginal Masculinities

> Now the woman's everywhere more than the man, you know?
> *JJ: Everywhere? In Egypt?*
> In Egypt, no. Because you're in Sinai. There is (sic) no women.
> *But there are women...*
> I mean this is the working area you know. So nobody born here and nobody live here. I mean no Egyptian is born here or lives here. So it start from now. Maybe in the next ten years you will find women. But not now... (Eid, 29, Dahab, September 2000).

In the previous chapters I argued that Western women who are involved in ethnosexual tourist-local relationships in the Sinai have certain geographical imaginations of place that inform and are informed by these encounters. These imaginations often consist of a reductionist form of cultural stereotyping that enables them to see and feel Sinai – and by engaging in relationships with its residents – as an escape from their personal experience of modernity. But this cultural stereotyping is not confined to just the women. Many men have also

Figure 5.2   Bedouin men making 'Bedouin tea' in the desert

Source: Jessica Jacobs (2000).

internalised these stereotypes and – as is often the case with dominant discourses – have reflected them back at the instigators.

It isn't necessarily stating the obvious to say that the gendering of Occidentalism and Orientalism is formed around ideas of racial difference. Or that racial difference is articulated through gender. Frankenberg notes how Western discourse on interracial relationships where the woman is white, can be more accurately described as a discourse 'against' interracial relationships:

> The *racialness* of constructions of masculinity and femininity are apparent in this discourse, as are the construction of race difference as 'real,' 'essential,' and based on 'biology' and the construction of racial and cultural groups as entirely and appropriately separate from one another (1993: 71).

Although most of the men I interviewed were very much in favour of interracial relationships (at least between them and white, Western women), the way in which the men I interviewed stressed their racial difference through essentialist notions of a form of hypermasculinity and sexual prowess can be seen as very similar to the expressions of racial difference within racial and culturally specific Third World stereotypes of masculinity.

The stereotypical nature of these masculinities can be seen by the limited variety of masculinities on offer (and expected); the apparent contradictions between the

**Figure 5.3   Young Egyptian men sit waiting for passing tourists. They often
work for shops and restaurants on a commission only salary**

Source: Jessica Jacobs (2000).

different versions (and often the inability to actually successfully produce these
masculinities in practice); and the lack of difference these contradictions made
to the expectations of the women and the continued expected performance of the
men.

If the Sinai is supposedly unmodern, premodern and antimodern, it is
unsurprising perhaps if masculinities that support this model are so sought after. We
have already heard how women like Marianne referred to (and preferred) Egyptian
and Bedouin men as 'real' men, unlike their European counterparts. Marianne told
me how this made everything more 'clear' compared to Europe where everything
was more 'in between'. This made it easier to be a woman, 'when you are with a
man in the Sinai' (Marianne, 39, Nuweiba, September 2000).

While the term 'real man' refers to Egyptians and Bedouins, the wilderness and
landscape of the Sinai is a crucial location for this masculinity. Such was the image
and appeal of Bedouin men (to women tourists at least) that it wasn't uncommon
for Egyptian men to participate in their own form of ethnomasquerade and dress to
fulfil women's desires for a gendered racial sexual fantasy of the Arab masculinity.
This could be achieved simply by dressing in a *galabeya* as opposed to say, jeans
and a t-shirt. Ashraf, 34, was married to a British woman and together they ran a

camp and restaurant in Dahab. Originally from the Nile Valley he was not averse to donning a *galabeya* and a *keffiyeh* when he took tourists on trips to the desert, especially if his group included young women. As we have seen, an image of Arab man in a *galabeya* was not only loaded with masculine sex appeal, for women like Susanne, it reinforced the authenticity of their experience and symbolised their spiritual connection with the landscape, proving they were at 'one with Nature' and therefore 'one with God'.

Joe, 26, was half American and half Bedouin, the son of a Jewish American artist and a Bedouin man she had met and married when she travelled in the Sinai in the 1970s. He was mostly brought up in Georgia in the USA with his younger brother, but moved back to the Sinai in his teens. He was very comfortable wearing either jeans and a t-shirt or a *galabeya*.

> If I don't wear my *galabeya*, the girls aren't interested. They don't want a Western guy, they want an Arab 'sheikh' (Joe, 23, Sharm El Sheikh, April 2000).

Unsurprisingly perhaps, most of the men I interviewed were pleased to accept and take on board these stereotypes of 'real' masculinity. As mentioned earlier, Amr had moved on from Dahab to Sharm El-Sheikh and changed his business from hiring out jetskis to renting motorbikes. For him (and his staff), work was a very successful way to meet women and they would often make arrangements to meet later in one of the bars and clubs in the popular nightlife strip in Na'ama Bay. Amr's comments were not that dissimilar to the statements from many women I interviewed: Western women came to Sinai because they were dissatisfied with European men and didn't find them 'manly' enough. And like Susanne he also made a direct racial comparison between Arab men and the racial stereotype of the hypersexuality of the black male. When Amr spoke about this quality however, the reference to sexual performance and stamina was more overt.

> Women complain sexually about European men.
>
> *JJ: What do they say?*
>
> Not good enough, not warm enough. Don't stay long. Maybe Egyptian men… is not black, is coloured, but not black. And at the same time is giving her a good time, stay long in bed. I mean you can't find European men staying a couple of hours or three or four hours and having sex, they won't do that. And they always (Egyptian men) want to do it all of the time. I mean they don't get fed up with that woman. They (European men) don't want to do it having sex all the time… (Amr, 28, Sharm El Sheikh, May 2000).

Egyptian men aren't 'black' exactly, he says, but he intimates they can provide the 'white' Western woman with a similarly satisfying experience. An experience that white Western men are unable to provide. With faint echoes of Bowman's revenge-seeking Palestinian shopkeepers, Amr is expressing a dualistic imagination of the economically powerful First World white man as hyposexual.

As we have seen in the previous chapter Egyptian/Bedouin men were also given another quality that differentiated them from other racial stereotypes of blackness and whiteness, namely a sensitivity that was presented as innately Arab. Egyptian men were 'gentlemen' while the ability of the Bedouin to embody the Sinai and Nature meant that, as this popular poem (see Figure 5.4) says they weren't just 'strong like the desert' they were also 'soft like the sea' and could 'walk like the wind'.

Hany, 37, was originally from Alexandria on the Mediterranean coast. He was a musician who had spent the last ten years playing the guitar in various hotel bars in Sharm El Sheikh and Nuweiba. He had been married to an Italian woman and lived in Italy for several years. He told me he was unhappy there however and had persuaded his wife and child to move back to the Sinai with him. But one day, he said, she disappeared with her daughter and returned back to Italy. I met Hany several years after this and at the time of the interview he had two foreign girlfriends, one Italian and one British (who came to the Sinai at different times). Hany also told me how Egyptian men were better lovers than Western men:

> It's the way I think that I make love with a girl. I'm so tender, you know. When
> I do make love with somebody, it's like – even (if it's for) one night – we touch
> more – maybe – and we speak good, sweet – we are more sweet than European
> men. That's what they tell me, it's not me (Hany 37, Nuweiba, April 2000).

When noting the appeal to women tourists of the 'romantic language' used by Jamaican men, Pruitt and LaFont (1995) suggest that the adoption of such language is part of a performance by the men who are attempting to fulfil the women's expectations of them as exotic lovers. They go on to propose that this allows the men to experiment with their identity by elaborating on their gender 'repertoire' in order to 'articulate the women tourists' idealisations of local culture and masculinity'. It is difficult to see how this gives the men an opportunity to experiment with their masculine identity when they are pandering to, and reinforcing the racial stereotypes. In addition this argument is based on an assumption that 'romantic language' is not a normal part of their 'repertoire' but in addition, this assumption certainly can't be made of the men in the Sinai who were convinced their sensitive attitude towards women and their 'romantic language' is very much a social norm in Egyptian society.

Hany's, and other men's, articulation of their local masculinity – whether it was their sensitivity, their sexual performance or being a 'real' man represented a double positioning that was used for two different purposes; they used it not only to compete with a (dominant) Western masculinity but also as a defence against some of the less positive stereotyping of the Arab male in the West.

According to Khaled the sexual appeal of Egyptian men did not play a significant part in the image women had before they came to the Sinai – in other words it was not a stereotype. Instead it was something they 'discovered' when

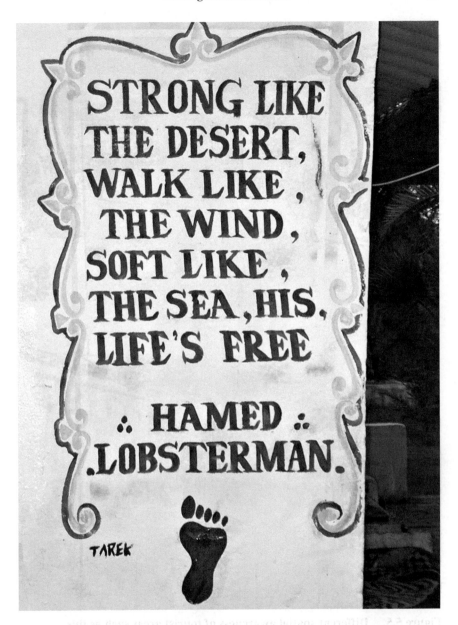

Figure 5.4 A popular 'poem' to the romance of Bedouin masculinity painted on the wall of a backpackers camp in Dahab stresses their sensitivity as well as their strength

Source: Jessica Jacobs (2000).

Figure 5.5   **Different spatial awareness of tourist areas such as this shopping street in Nuweiba (Tarrabin) mean European women tourists often think nothing of wearing bikinis away from the beach. The resulting attention from Egyptian men is sometimes welcomed, at other times classified as 'harassment'**

Source: Jessica Jacobs (2000).

they arrived. The stereotype they had was a politically-oriented negative image of Arab men, created by jealous (and sexually inferior) Western men.

> They think that Egyptians are maniacs, this is what they think and this is what they have been told. But I always believe that if the woman or the girl is smart enough, she has to discover by herself (Khaled, 28, Sharm El Sheikh, August 2000).

According to Khaled, once women discovered for themselves how nice Egyptian men were, they kept coming back. In this way the ethnosexual tourist-local encounters between Egyptian men and Western women do not reinforce (negative) gendered racial and sexual stereotypes of the Other, they contest them. Or to put it another way, the discourses within these encounters hold the potential to deconstruct pre-existing notions of marginal masculinity:

> After, they come back for the people. But the first time no, because they don't know how the Egyptian does. So when they come they change. Now you look most the Italians are married to Egyptian. Most of the Swiss and German are married to Egyptians. They are leaving [Europe] and coming up [to Sinai]. That means that the climate was an attraction before the Egyptian. The next time they come for the Egyptian, in the sense, I mean if they like somebody. But the first time, no, they are not coming for the Egyptian. You never know the Egyptian how they are. They come and discover that the Egyptian are gentle, very nice with hospitality, so they start to think OK we have nice people, nice weather, so why not again. And then the story starts (Khaled, 28, Sharm El Sheikh, August 2000).

While it is not a typical Western ideal of manliness, it was obviously important for Egyptian men to be seen as romantic, sensitive and caring to women if they wanted to consider themselves 'real men'. Amr told me that Western women come to Sinai just to be noticed and treated like an attractive 'woman' because they didn't get this kind of attention in Europe:

> She feel a woman. European women here they feel like real... I mean because in Europe nobody cares. I mean, you can walk into a place full of men and nobody notice that you're walking there. You know what I mean? Here you walk in the street and everybody is telling you about your beautiful ass and your beautiful body going round, your beautiful eyes, I want to marry you or whatever. You really feel like somebody... (Amr, 28, Sharm El Sheikh, May 2000).

Many women told me of the expectation that they would be harassed by men in Egypt. One of the most common stereotypes of the Arab man is a lecherous male who can't keep his hands off 'white' women. When I was a travel writer for the *Rough Guides* young women often asked me whether it was safe for single white women to travel in the Middle East and how to avoid harassment from men who misunderstand liberal Western women and think they are all sexually available. Yet Amr here is suggesting that women come to Sharm El Sheikh specifically to find this kind of stereotypical behaviour. They seek out such 'harassment'.[2] The atmosphere in Sharm El Sheikh is certainly affected by the fact that all tourist women receive sexual attention from the 'locals' in some form or other, intimidating some women but perhaps appealing to others.

I asked Amr why he thought the Egyptian men who live and work in Sharm El Sheikh behaved like that towards the women tourists. His answer included a variety of reasons that focused on 'difference':

> Because it's different. It's different. I think it's the food, or the heat around. I mean I don't know. These guys can screw up women day and night. Doesn't matter. For Egyptian men, European girls are really nice… they are very different. You have blond women, white and really nice bodies and dressing in sexy things, which they don't really see in Egypt (Amr, 28, Sharm El Sheikh, May 2000).

Amr is incorporating Western (Occidental if you like) racial and sexual stereotypes of the Orient and black cultures into his explanation. Egyptian men are hot blooded because they come from a hot country and eat hot food. This means they have great sexual stamina and also think about sex all the time.

The women he talks about are being othered and exoticised through this imagination of difference. They are also primarily described as 'bodies', and defined through the body. They are attractive because of their 'difference' and their most obvious difference is again related to their body, because they are white.

The argument that Middle Eastern women are seen to embody their culture, religion and tradition has been made by Moghadam (1993) and Kandyoti (1991) among others, who point out it is the women, not the men who are expected to dress in clothes that represent their culture, while most men are able to alternate between Western and 'traditional' clothing. Women in the West can also be said to act as representatives of Western culture, of 'modernity' through the body, and especially by what they wear, and don't wear. Significantly Amr points out the colour of the women's hair and skin, their visibility of their body, and the emphasis women place on their sexuality through their clothing.

But it is not only the difference between Egyptian (and Bedouin) women and Western women that is appealing, it is the association these women have with Western values and lifestyles, with modernity that an Occidental geographical imagination puts great value on. An association that is primarily made through the body.

---

2   It must be said that Amr was a wealthy, well-educated and good looking young man who liked to spend a lot of money on his 'girls'. His advances are therefore likely to be more happily received perhaps than if they come from other quarters.

Amr's next comment reflects many of these attitudes and practices. He tells me about one period in his life when he shared his luxury apartment with seven women of differing nationalities. One evening, he said, they all ended up in bed together:

> Yeah, I had Russians, German, French, Egyptian, Scandinavian, English, it was unbelievable. But believe me it's very nice. I mean when you have six, seven kind of culture in the shape of a woman; that one with big tits, that one nice ass, that one with very nice legs, that one with very nice colour of body, this one blond, this one dark-haired, they are all together... (Amr, 28, Sharm El Sheikh, May 2000).

Here Amr stresses the physicality of the women – their breasts, their bottoms, legs and their colour, almost as if he could take one component from each and make up the perfect 'woman' and therefore the perfect country or culture to live in. But his point that 'culture' is 'in the shape of the woman' shows how these women's bodies represent the modernity from where they have come. Crucially, however, Amr's masculine gaze allows him to act as the subject and focus of it all. He is the reason the women are there, as a man he is in control of the situation. Whether or not this event actually took place is not important. The different cultures and societies of mostly Western countries are embodied in these women's bodies, and by controlling them through his masculinity he can feel in control of his relationship with the wider and usually more dominant world.

The association of masculinity and sexual appeal with the desert is also not just confined to European women, but incorporated into the geographical imaginations of the men, many of whom are also coming from crowded urban areas elsewhere in Egypt. We are back with Amr again. Here he tells me how romantic the desert and the sea are, even if he finds it difficult to explain why at first:

> I don't know. I don't know. I mean when you go in the desert or on a boat, you stay in that place with that guy with a candle, having some wine. Anything can happen. Even if you're married and you're having ten kids, you won't resist that. Especially in the desert, I mean with all the reputation you have about the desert (Amr, 28, Sharm El Sheikh, May 2000).

Amr is obviously influenced by geographical imaginations of the desert and its 'reputation', showing how sexualised desert metaphors are not confined to Western society. The critically acclaimed Egyptian film *Sleeping in Honey* (dir. Sherif Arafa, Ali Idrees 1996) [El Noom fi el Asal], starring Adel Imam, uses the desert as a metaphor to comment on a perceived crisis in masculinity caused by modernity; in this case life in the city of Cairo. The main character is a policeman investigating a murder. The stress of city life leaves him impotent and he finds he can only make love to his wife when they go to spend the night in the desert. Here landscape is used to comment on sexuality and identity, but without incorporating Western Orientalist stereotypes of the 'other'. Amr goes on to expand on the reputation of the desert; the desert is 'sex', it is a connection with an awesome nature that is achieved through sex with a 'local' man. Amr puts himself in the position of the woman he is with and imagines how she feels in the desert, with her man:

> It's power. You feel it. You feel it. Did you ever feel that when you stayed in the desert and the rocks that surround you are alive? It's a very strong feeling and sometimes it stays with me. In that particular moment with that guy, that you really want to get wild in that minute. Curled around on that sand naked, pull over whatever, it's just a feeling that you can't resist, even if you have a boyfriend you really love or husband. You won't resist on that moment. You will just wait for the first move he will do and you will do it all (Amr, 28, Sharm El Sheikh, May 2000).

In Soueif's *The Map of Love* (1999) the first love story that is 'mapped' out is intertwined with the Egyptian hero's desire for modernisation in order to overthrow the British occupiers. But it is interpreted, as this is a romantic novel, through gender and the institution of marriage, where Egyptian and European women symbolise culture and are contrasted. Egyptian women represent tradition and the aristocratic travelling English woman modernity. The nationalist hero, Sharif al-Baroudi explains to his mother why he has returned his Egyptian bride to her father and lays the groundwork toward finding – and falling in love with – a suitable foreign woman from a 'modern' country:

> *Ya Ummi*, I cannot live my life with a woman who has no key to my mind and who does not share my concerns. She cannot – will not – read anything. She shrugs off the grave problems of the day and asks if I think her new tablecloth is pretty…I need my partner to be someone to whom I can turn, confident of her sympathy, believing her when she tells me I'm in the wrong, strengthened when she tells me I'm in the right. I want to love and be loved back – but what I see is not love or companionship but a sort of transaction of convenience, sanctioned by religion and society and I do not want it (1999: 151).

Marriage itself has been modernised. It is no longer a 'transaction of convenience sanctioned by religion and society', it is a transaction of mutual love. And love itself here is modernised too: love is a sort of companionship, a meeting of minds, a friendship with support and mutual respect. Sharif al-Baroudi therefore chooses a foreign woman as his bride because she represents modernity – the way forward – and eschews an Egyptian woman as a wife because she represents tradition, the 'premodern' and therefore marriage to her would mean taking a step backward. Marriage becomes an institution of change, an institution to be used as a bridge toward modernity that aims to avoid some of the conflict and trials bound up with other options that would also lead to modernity. Marriage to a foreign woman incorporates gender power relations in an attempt to balance the inequity of First/ Third World relations.

Sharif is still seeking marriage within a patriarchal structure and this should ensure the masculine remains in control. He is not going to lose power to this symbol of modernity because this symbol is a woman, not a man.

Some of the men I have interviewed gave similar rationales for preferring to engage in relationships with European women. Several Egyptian men stated they preferred relationships with European women to those with Egyptian women precisely because they felt they could be companions, because they could talk to them about all sorts of subjects. In this imagination then, Western women were not just bodies representing modernity, but minds. They could engage in modernity in a non-threatening way.

Hassan, 32, worked as a DJ in Na'ama Bay and was engaged to a Swiss woman when I interviewed him. In a parallel development to the idea of women travelling as 'honorary men', Hassan and other Egyptian men saw Western women as 'equals' in that their racial privilege was cancelled out by their gender. They could therefore be 'friends' with European women because cultural restrictions did not count:

> I like them intelligent. Because I think there is no distance between me and them when I talk. They can understand me. It's like a doctor, whatever this is a girl or a boy, I find the distance like I'm friendly with them and they are friendly with me. I think if I'm going to talk with Egyptian girl maybe she's embarrass me – you know what I mean? Maybe she is quite close, maybe she thinks something else. So I close the road, like I don't want to try. Like I don't even if there is something good, but OK I finished the road, no Egyptian woman in my life (Hassan, 32, Sharm El Sheikh, April 2000).

According to Hassan, because Egyptian social exchange between single men and women was restricted, any social contact with an Egyptian woman would be taken as a form of courtship. He thought women in Egypt were so fixated on romance that if you spoke to one they thought you were in love and wanted to get married. Jamal felt the same way about Bedouin women:

> I'm working here. It's easy to find someone, some friends and talk to them, even if I don't have a relationship with a girl, so I can talk to her about anything. You know people...here in Egypt...I mean if I meet a (Bedouin) girl and talk to her together, nobody else, and anybody saw us, so it would be different. They say you have a relationship or something like that (Jamal, 25, Sharm El Sheikh, April 2000).

Some men mentioned other deterrents to establishing a relationship with a 'local' woman, such as the expense involved in marrying an Egyptian woman compared to marrying a 'foreign' woman because it was the responsibility of the man to provide a house and all furniture before the marriage. In contrast, a relationship with a European woman removed this obstacle and could also, of course, mean the man's financial position improved significantly. However the men I interviewed rarely alluded to this directly, unless they were talking about other men, as no-one wanted to admit financial considerations played a part in their choice of partner; whether this meant they could not afford to marry an Egyptian woman, or marrying a foreign woman held economic advantages.

Conclusion

In many ways modernity was seen as a feminising influence, especially in view of the fact that, many men felt their most direct involvement with modernity was through Western women. The positionality of Egyptians and Bedouins in terms of masculinity was often presented in a similar way to the European women. Men I spoke to often referred to themselves as 'real' men in relation to European men, offering proof in the fact that it was European women who came to them.

Local men also used racialised and sexualised stereotypes in their geographical imaginations of Europe and European women, and incorporated and played up to the women's stereotypes of them. European women's representation through the body and their potential power as First Worlders often led to an ambivalent attitude to European women. On the one hand they were treated like queens – as Susanne told me of her experience in Egypt – yet on the other hand they were stereotyped and criticised for their overt sexual behaviour. Men like Amr, who lived in the tourist resorts of Sinai, were faced with women coming every day, many of whom were looking for sex or relationships with them. Stereotypes of Western women were not difficult to construct in the Sinai. As Amr told me:

> Just look at them, they are looking for sex. Easy women. Some of them don't
> care about which guy they go with. Just want to have a good time…She just
> want a brown body… (Amr, 28, Sharm El Sheikh, May 2000).

It wasn't difficult for men new to Sharm El Sheikh to conclude that all women tourists were looking for sex, although this did tend to recede over time.

Today, Said's Orientalism is often seen as a problematic term that, despite owing so much to feminist theory, still fails to incorporate gender into its analysis. Once possible reason for this oversight might be that the additional layer of gender complicates Orientalism, exposing ambivalence and inconsistencies and revealing new power relations. Egyptian and Bedouin men can be seen to be exhibiting Occidental geographical imaginations by incorporating Orientalist stereotypes into their behaviour with women and mixing in a few of their own stereotypes about European women. While they do not imagine the Sinai or themselves as premodern, unmodern and antimodern in the same way as the women – they have adopted certain stereotypes surrounding masculinity that incorporate the women's geographical imaginations, stereotypes that are seen to work in their favour and use imaginations of the desert and the beach that support this gendered identity. Modernity is also situated differently by the men. To some extent it is imagined as a Western condition not an Egyptian one, found in Europe and embodied in European women tourists, but it is also very much thought to exist in the resorts of the Sinai as well as the urban spaces of Cairo (in a less attractive form). While the Bedouin are imagined as premodern, unmodern and antimodern by some men, the resorts with their luxury hotels, Western lifestyles, restaurants and bars are in contrast very much viewed as 'ultramodern' and I will examine the spatial aspects of tourist modernity in Chapter 6. By moving from other parts of Egypt to the Sinai, and becoming involved with European women, they do not intend to 'escape' from modernity, but to engage with it on more favourable terms.

Chapter 6
Negotiations in Tourist Space

The production of separate dichotomous zones/spaces of order and desire has long been associated with the establishment and practice of both colonialism and modernity. Tourism, as practised by Western workers, generally belongs to the space of desire, and is separated from places of work temporally and spatially. Spaces for leisure, particularly tourist zones, are usually found far away from modern spaces of labour (except of course for those who work in tourism) – normally the further away the better and more status-enhancing the experience. Different landscapes to the ones we are familiar with, especially those laden with historical imaginaries suit this purpose very well – and the most popular tourist destinations tend to be those that manage to combine these salient features with a strong relationship formed during colonialism, a good climate and nice beaches.

Egypt has perhaps the longest history of international package tourism in the world, thanks to Thomas Cook. 'The original top 10 holiday destinations' in *The Guardian* newspaper (2009) invites the reader to 'step back in time' to when 'tourism as we know it had been born' and lists the Nile River cruise that Cook established as the most popular holiday destination for Victorian travellers in the late nineteenth century. As we have seen the maintenance of a successful tourist imaginary of place in Egypt (and many other formerly colonised regions of the world) as desirable (and therefore a commodity that people are willing to pay for) relies to a great degree in the marketing and exploitation of this nostalgia for early tourism in its reproduction and expression. This process is not confined to the production of marketing literature or the personal geographical imaginations of tourists and the toured, but is also found in the production of tourist space.

Tourist space is often sub-divided up into two contrasting categories, the informal and the formal. In the Sinai the Bedouin/backpacker tourist village of Dahab and the Bedouin camps in Nuweiba would, in general, qualify as what Edensor calls 'heterogeneous' tourist space (1998) while the hotel dominated resort of Sharm El Sheikh is closer to what he has termed 'enclavic' tourist space (1998: 42).

In this chapter I will explore some of the connections between the tourist spaces of the Sinai and the relationships that Western women and local men that take place there. While these terms (particularly enclavic tourist space) certainly reflect attempts by the neoliberal elements of the tourist industry to control the borders of the spaces of leisure in the Sinai, they do not help to describe the complexity of tourist space in the Sinai, or provide an adequate framework for the relationships and encounters that occur there.

Touring Tourist Space

Tourist space is capable of generating huge revenues for investors, but to do this it needs to be heavily regulated in both its production and its maintenance particularly concerning the maintenance of its borders. Many tourist zones can be in messy places where different spaces intersect, making the regulation of tourist space more difficult to enforce, and to observe. However, in the south Sinai the borders are relatively clearly defined due to the almost complete absence of social and cultural life outside of tourism. And, if those borders are encroached upon – as in the case of the bomb attacks in Sharm El Sheikh and Dahab in 2005 and 2006 – the state can quickly intervene to shore up these borders with extra checkpoints and the construction of physical barriers like concrete walls.

Until the 1980s the Sinai was a sparsely populated region – apart from the military presence (international and national) – the majority of the population were Bedouins whose presence was (and is) low key, mostly consisting of small houses and farms, desert tracks, camels, sheep, goats, jeeps and Toyoto pick-ups. The industry of tourism is a recent event that is directly or indirectly responsible for just about everything else that has come to the Sinai subsequently[1] – such as the airport, the dive boats, the marina, roads, hotels, shops, petrol stations, restaurants, diving centres, landscaped gardens, beach furniture, watersports, tour companies, tour buses, quadrunners, swimming pools and so on. Even the Egyptian government housing, shops and other facilities not meant for tourists have developed from a need to house people who have moved to the area to work in the tourist sector.

While the Sinai is a relatively large area, it is also mountainous and tourist space is mostly confined to the coast. In her work on the effect of tourism development on the local populations, Aziz (1999) divided the Sinai into three main geographical spaces – the Interior, the Road and the Coast – allocating each area to a different set of actors in the Sinai. Thus the desert interior is the prime territory of the Bedouin; anyone that ventures there can only do so with their help and permission. The roads, with their checkpoints, are the state and represent the Egyptian government's control of movement between the interior and the coast. The third space – the coast – is the prime space of interaction between Egyptians, Bedouins and tourists and, as Aziz notes, each group has 're-constructed the landscape of the Coast in their own way – to reflect their own objectives' (1999: 173). However, the success of this 'reconstruction' also depends on the degree of power each group has to realise their aims.

According to Edensor, formal or 'enclavic' tourist space is organised, requires large amounts of capital investment, and is constructed to international tourist standards. The necessary capital comes from international business, aid agencies

---

1   While much of the military presence in the Sinai is there to protect these highly valuable tourist assets and the Egyptian president when he visits, elements such as the MFO (Multinational Force and Observers) also reflect the Sinai's geopolitical importance as a buffer zone with Israel and Gaza.

and the state and the focus is on creating, and maintaining Western-style products with Western levels of service. Hotels have landscaped gardens and internal spaces such as restaurants and lobbies are created with a 'monitored aesthetic' – where 'ideals of cleanliness and just a hint of the "exotic" concoct the requisite combination of high standards and strangeness'. We have already seen examples of this with the generic naming of hotels in Sharm El Sheikh and the way in which they attempt to link these buildings with romantic colonial heydays and popular notions of a beach paradise. According to Edensor this 'theming' imposes a visual order effectively creating a 'spatial economic and cultural circuit to the exclusion of other local commercial enterprises' (1998: 46).

The ever-expanding resort of Sharm El Sheikh with its multiplicity of international hotel chains meets many of the criteria of the enclave. As do the resort areas in Dahab and between Nuweiba and Taba in the north near the border with Israel. According to Edensor enclavic tourist space is constructed to resemble model towns where there is no litter, no crime and it is easy to stroll everywhere and meet other people. These spaces are 'designed to stimulate desires: to escape, to meet 'others' and to transgress'; they are places designed for freedom, although they are also so controlled that,

> ...the possibilities for transgressing, experiencing sensual richness and confronting difference are sharply delimited by the ordering processes that dominate (1998: 47–8).

The main tourist centre of Sharm El Sheikh in Na'ama Bay is certainly designed to encourage such sociality through strolling. A corniche (beachfront walkway) stretches from one end of Na'ama Bay to the other connecting all the hotels to the beach, while a parallel pedestrianised street lies behind these hotels, full of open-air cafés and restaurants perfect for what the Italians call the 'passagiata' (evening stroll).

In contrast, Edensor defines heterogeneous tourist spaces as areas that 'accommodate tourism as one economic activity but are not dominated by it' (1998: 54). Heterogeneous tourist spaces are overlapping and multi-functional and usually located within market or bazaar areas where boundaries between public and private are blurred (to Western eyes at least). In the Sinai this would correspond to the downtown area of Sharm El Sheikh and the Bedouin tourist areas of Dahab and Nuweiba (Asilah and Tarrabin).

This kind of tourist space gives the tourist an opportunity to move through a kind of space that is regulated in a different way. Here is the desired 'richly sensual encounter' where,

> ... there is little descent into deference, and as tourists and locals must mingle with each other, the opportunities for meeting locals are part of the tourist experience (1998: 55).

Figure 6.1   The seemingly innocuous low cement wall that runs between the city of Sharm El Sheikh and the nearby desert serves to separate the local Bedouin community from the tourist space of Sharm El Sheikh and restricts their movement to formal roads with checkpoints

Source: Jessica Jacobs (2010).

However the Sinai differs from the enclaves Edensor describes in several ways. Firstly Sinai's tourist enclaves aren't spaces designed solely for foreign (Western) tourists; the resort of Sharm El Sheikh and resort areas in Nuweiba/Taba and Dahab are not only very popular with Arab tourists from elsewhere in the region, but also a burgeoning Egyptian middle class and this is reflected in their style and atmosphere.

Secondly the south Sinai as a whole is an enclave, a peninsula cut off from the rest of Egypt geographically by the Red Sea and the Suez Canal and geopolitically through the control of roads by the Egyptian government. Although most tourists don't notice because they can pass unchecked, access to the Sinai enclave (particularly for lower class Egyptians and Bedouins) is heavily controlled by military checkpoints and a branch of the state machine dedicated to the control of relations between the tourist and the local – the Tourist Police.

The borders of the tourist spaces of the Sinai have been more heavily controlled since the bomb attacks on Dahab and Sharm El Sheikh in 2005 and 2006. In 2007 these barriers became more physically visible – the checkpoint before Sharm El Sheikh now charges entry to non-residents and a low cement wall separates Sharm El Sheikh from the surrounding Bedouin settlements.

Edensor's enclaves are presented as clearly bounded with access denied to locals who 'may spend their work-time here, but rarely their leisure time' (1998: 47). In the Sinai, 'locals' who work there come from elsewhere in Egypt. They often work 12–16 hours a day for 28 days with the following eight days off. While they might return to their homes (in Cairo or elsewhere in Egypt) for the eight free days, they are obliged to spend the rest of their free time in the enclave.

Because the whole of Sinai is an enclave, the so-called heterogeneous places lie within the enclave and are just as manufactured as the resort spaces as we shall see in the next section. The gated villa complexes might be 'guests only' but limited access is possible to their shops and between these spaces, there are a number of more open zones (still within the enclave) where it is possible to spend your free time as a consumer – places like the downtown market, the shopping malls and the restaurants, cafes and bars outside the resorts. Indeed these mixed tourist-local spaces of the Sinai and the ability to traverse them and encounter tourists is a major part of the attraction of working in the region and offer opportunities to experience a lifestyle unavailable elsewhere in the country.

Edensor and others might refer to these spaces as heterogeneous, because they are located near to the enclave and are supposedly more cluttered, disorganised and give more access to the 'real' Egypt.

However in the Sinai, all tourist space is enclavic and tourism remains dominant, even in the Bedouin village of Asilah in Dahab, tourism dominates and the village has progressively moved further along (and away from) the coast to accommodate tourist development.

Finally, while the Sinai's international tourist resorts have a globalised aesthetic and share many features, the regulatory attempts to commodify, regulate and privatise tourist space is not always uniform, nor complete. Tourists and locals mingle everywhere – whether they are in their luxury resort being served cocktails by a waiter or shopping in the bazaars, encounters are constantly taking place. Opportunities for women tourists to transgress or 'experience sensual richness' and 'confront difference' through ethnosexual relationships with locals are no less likely to occur on the beaches of Sharm El Sheikh than they are in the Bedouin camps in Nuweiba.

Interestingly, while heterogeneous tourist space is often situated next to large enclavic spaces, the relationship between the two remains relatively unexplored. Enclavic and heterogeneous tourist space as formal and informal spaces of experience, are instead set up in a binary of opposition – one is supposedly bounded and permanent while the other remains somehow permeable. However these categories, in the south Sinai at least, are far more fluid and overlapping than this categorisation suggests. Enclavic tourist space is an important categorisation, but more for what it represents to the tourist and the tourist worker. For the locals these gated villa and resort complexes represent modernity, often seen as alien to local culture. And while for some visitors the modernity of the enclavic tourist resort is so unattractive anything will be done to avoid these places, for others they are the main destination.

If their gateway status means that, in practice, tourist enclaves are hard to avoid; it is here you will find the physical as well as symbolic portals, in the form of airports, bus stations and taxis. The concentration of technologies in these spaces of modernity or hypermodernity means they are usually required at some point by all travellers. Workers, both foreign and more local workers, need to use the same bus and air transport network that tourists use (although most hotels also provide staff transport). And all leisured mobility requires constant maintenance and constant consumption. Even if traveller tourists are eschewing modernity to go and live in the desert, the resources of the enclave of Sharm El Sheikh are still necessary to maintain this mobility and support people's existence when they are away from home. Technologies such as internet cafes, satellite television; tour operators so they can book flights home; the recompression diving chamber and diving equipment if they are divers, the bus and taxi service to Cairo; the luxury hotels that so many travellers treat themselves with in between roughing it, and so on.

Most short-term visits to the Sinai, whether in travelling or tourist mode, might involve a mixed use of the different spaces on offer but in many ways they follow a similar chronology and ritual of performance where the itinerary starts and ends in Sharm El Sheikh or the fancier hotels in Dahab and Nuweiba. This is partly because visitors mostly enter and depart from these points but there are other factors. The desert safari takes you far away from civilisation for a few days or perhaps a week but mostly it is ended by one night in a four or five star hotel in order for the tourist to appreciate and enjoy the trappings of a kind of 'intermediate' exotic modernity after being briefly removed from such comforts as a buffet dinner, satellite television, a swimming pools and hot showers. Even travellers who generally reject the enclavic setup of the resort feel justified in enjoying it for one or two nights if they have first suffered to some extent beforehand. Every year, Luisa, 42, left her husband and children in Germany to spend a week in the desert alone, with only one or two Bedouin visiting her with supplies. But at the beginning – and more importantly the end – she always spent a few days in a hotel with a bar that was close to the beach.

> It's nice to get away in the desert. But it's also very nice to come back here (the hotel) for a beer! (Luisa, 42, Sharm El Sheikh, September 2000).

Enclavic tourist space as a category seems restricted in its usefulness by expectations that it is clearly delineated, so that it is everything that 'heterogeneous' tourist space is not.

To separate enclavic from heterogeneous space for the purposes of categorisation tends to valorise one over the other, in much the same vein that travelling has offered itself as superior to tourism ever since this form of categorisation began in the late nineteenth century (or even before). For Edensor there is a value in 'transgressing', 'experiencing sensual richness' and 'confronting difference'; but it is unclear how desirable this outcome is, and perhaps most important, in whose interest. If not looked at questioningly, these aims to transgress, to confront difference and to experience sensuality in the heterogeneous zones – can just be another one-sided way of 'othering', another form of the consumption of out of time exoticism (and rejection of their modernity) by Western travellers/tourists travelling in the Third World.

Edensor's categories seem to be placing the tourists in two possible positionalities or binaries – either they form part of the civilisation and modernity from which they come – or they attempt to escape it in order to experience some form of 'authentic' sensual experience of 'otherness.' Incorporating Urry's tourist gaze, Edensor argues the 'design-led regeneration, uncluttered spaces, smooth surfaces and carefully placed artworks' (2007: 219) of highly regulated tourist space (and indeed Western modernity in general) means that other senses that are stimulated through touch, sound, and smell are suppressed so that visitors are visually able to 'take possession of objects and environments, often at a distance' (Urry 2002: 147).

There is a definite delineation between the enclavic and heterogeneous that also seems to reflect ideas of 'natural' or 'authentic' as opposed to the artifice of the enclave. Furthermore while one is 'clean' and therefore wiped of meaning, the other is given the richness of all the sights and smells of the 'exotic'.

> ...it seems that the sensual and social body passing through heterogeneous tourist space is continually imposed upon and challenged by diverse activities, sensations and sights which render a state at variance with the restrained and distanced distraction of the tourist enclave (1998: 59).

The possibility to supplement the tourist gaze with other senses put forward by Edensor is very valuable. However to give one tourist space this quality of 'diverse tactile sensations' and 'smellscapes' but deny the other seems unfair, and as I have argued, the assumption that unorganised tourist space is somehow more authentic or allows visitors greater access still needs to be looked at within the context of the role that heterogeneous tourist space plays in reinforcing exoticising stereotypes of place and people.

In his study of Kathmandu, Leichty (1996) refrains from separating tourist space into two distinct categories, instead referring to the multi-layered aspects of tourist spaces, which are 'overpopulated with places'. Tourist spaces exist in a world that has become increasingly 'deterritorialized' and where imaginations are 'increasingly mass-mediated and "liberated" from the confines of the locale'. This approach allows for the fact that geographical imaginations of places can become part of tourist's memories well before they ever set foot in the place – from media such as postcards, films, documentaries, newspaper stories, even just from meeting people who have been there.[2] In this way, tourist spaces are 'denotive hot spots, zones of complex images and imaginary hyperactivity' characterised by,

---

2   Leichty refers to a comment by David Morley and Kevin Robins in 'No Place like *Heimat*: Images of Home(land) (1995): '(I)dentity, memory and nostalgia – are inextricably

...complex conditions for the production and reproduction of locality in which...
work, business, and leisure weave together various circulating populations with
various kinds of 'locals'...As transitory, commercialised, even liminal zones,
these are spaces in which the controlled management of meaning is next to
impossible (1996: 101).

Leichty's 'translocalities' most closely correspond to Edensors 'heterogeneous'
and Aziz's 'Coastal' tourist space. However Liechty, incorporating the impact
of geographical imaginations upon shared spaces, describes a slightly different
encounter taking place.

As sites that carry a heavy imaginary burden, spaces such as these might be
instances of what Marshall Berman calls 'modern environments' and what
Renato Rosaldo calls 'border zones'. According to Rosaldo, the 'border' is a
'zone between stable places', the 'site of the implosion of the Third World into
the first,' On the other hand the locations described in this essay are perhaps
zones in which the First World implodes into the third (1996: 100).

Leichty's translocalities are spaces used by a cross-section of Nepalese society and
a variety of tourists. Here they interact, and play roles 'in a space where multiple
imaginations of 'others' meet'.

These are simultaneously places that foreigners imagine from a distance and
sites from which Nepalis imagine distant places. Just as films, travel books and
newspapers have helped to produce the memories of Kathmandu that tourists bring
with them to Nepal, Nepalis also have mediated memories of other places and
seek to live other lives by inhabiting these liminal spaces. In these semantically
unstable zones people are relatively free to enact the scripts and roles playing in
their own imaginations – even if a political economy of places (mirrored in the
pathways of global tourism) guarantees that most Nepalis will only experience
'flights' of the imagination. Thus these translocalities are often highly dramatic,
performative spaces in which both tourists and Nepalis experiment with identities
and practices that would be inappropriate in other locations where the meaning of
place is more rigidly controlled (1996: 101–2).

As Leichty notes of the Nepalese tourist town of Thamel, tourists are helped in
their scriptwriting by those working in the tourist industry.

Constantly scanning tourist's imagined scripts, Thamel business people are
quick to create suitable stages and props through which different tourists can
live out a variety of romantic dramas (1996: 108).

---

interlinked with patterns and flows of communication. The memory banks of our times are
in some part built out of the materials supplied by the film and television industries'.

Leichty's 'stages and props' complement the tourist's geographical imaginations. The Sinai offers stages for performance with tropical beaches, a vast desert and props like date palms and camels. As I have argued, the ritual of going on holiday sets up geographical imaginations that are so necessary for the tourists to enjoy the place and space they travel to. Leichty gives an example of what happens if you travel without this imaginary homework with an account of two American male tourists lying on a beach in Thailand impulsively decide to go to Kathmandu after seeing a leaflet float by. They travel without a pre-imagined idea of what it might be like and instead of seeing it as the romantic place that it has become in many tourists imaginations, they just see the pollution and poverty.

> ...we live in an age in which, in a matter of days, on a whim, two North Americans can find themselves in a remote Nepali hill village in a befuddled daze. But...I was also struck by the way in which tourists arriving with no preparation or forethought are unshielded from the facts of Nepali poverty and underdevelopment. Al and Gus had not carried out the preliminary imaginative labor necessary to transform Kathmandu into the nonhistorical and classless *place of their dreams*. All of us work to construct places – both 'our own' and 'others'; we work to imagine and naturalize difference; and we work to maintain and inhabit these fictions of place. But for tourists, those who must transport their sensibilities and dreams through space, the labor of producing places is a task of particularly heroic proportions. Without this prefiguring labor, Kathmandu was an abomination (1996: 110).

While Egypt can hardly be considered nonhistorical as a tourist destination, it remains the case that the history that is produced for the consumption of Western visitors – the requisite 'prefiguring labour' is highly selective and relies on a colonial history as interpreted by travel writers. Many other histories – local histories, Islamic history, even its most recent history and its own modernity – are often heavily edited or abruptly left out of the tourist destination equation. And, as in the case of many destinations, Egyptians are often presented as a homogenous group of people, categorised perhaps by their urban or regional status but rarely by other more 'modern' categories such as 'class'. The work of the tourist imagination is as important as the labour of the construction arm of the global tourist industry in dreaming these tourist places into being.

According to Edensor only enclavic tourist spaces are 'non-places'. The rest is somehow real. Yet, Liechty contends that travel writers have created a Nepal where the whole country has been written as a place of non-history – inviting tourists to replace local history with their own fantasies of place. While Egypt has a long and distinguished history, it is so vast (and colonially selective) it almost becomes timeless; certainly ancient and therefore able to connect us to prehistory. But it is never allowed to be modern, or, on the rare occasions that it is allowed, its modernity is never endowed with the traumatic break with the past that Western modernity is. This allows visitors to place their fantasies of place onto the people and landscape, even in resorts like Sharm El Sheikh despite its newness.

Sharm El Sheikh might be a 'non-place' in that it did not exist before the tourist industry created it; but as tourist space, like the other tourist spaces in the Sinai, it has been built upon geographical imaginations of the previous sites of encounters between Westerners and 'natives'. Edensor notes that,

> ...in many post-colonial settings, organised tourist space takes over the old colonial quarters, reproducing the old distinction between western colonialists and 'natives' and circumscribing appropriate spaces for each (1998: 47).

Despite Sinai having such a long and varied history, the history available to the tourist/traveller about the Sinai is remarkably limited and often written backwards. One of the most obvious examples of this is 'downtown' Sharm El Sheikh, which is also an example of how informal tourist space can be just as constructed and suppressed as the more formal spaces it appears next to. Downtown Sharm is a seemingly haphazard clutter of shops, bazaars, restaurants and stalls opposite a beach that used to be the main marina in the 1990s. It offers tourists all the sensuous experiences that Edensor associates with trangression (and authenticity?). At the beginning of 2001, this area was re-zoned and renamed 'The Old Market', with a large concrete gateway erected (see Figure 6.2). The only shops allowed were those that reflected tourist expectations of a old city 'bazaar' much like the *Khan El Khalili* tourist market in Cairo. Today most visitors to the resort believe that this heterogeneously cluttered yet completely designed area is the old part of the town of Sharm El Sheikh in keeping with geographical imaginations of tourist destinations where the tourist 'enclave' is located next to a site of historical significance or old quarter.

Points of Arrival

Within the same tourist space there are different places occurring at the same time depending on the positionality of the person. According to Liechty, for Indians Kathmandu is,

> ...an off-shore island of glitzy cosmopolitan consumer excess where visitors can live out fantasy roles as big spenders and high rollers, even while for many Western and East Asian tourists the city has precisely the opposite ethos, of oriental spirituality, exoticism, and ascetic simplicity (1996: 110).

Sinai too has many different, contrasting meanings. For many Egyptian families a trip to Sharm El Sheikh is like a visit to a theme park or film set as the resort and nearby desert panoramas are used in countless glamorous Egyptian movies and pop videos. With its five star international hotels and abundance of international visitors it is an adventure into a lifestyle of jetset luxury and glamour. Yet for Western visitors it is supposed to be – among other things – the Orient in all its

Figure 6.2   The gleaming new gateway to Sharm El Sheikh's 'Old Market' – a motley collection of souvenir shops in warehouses built in the late 1990s

Source: Jessica Jacobs (2002).

sensual splendour, the mysterious wonders of the Red Sea, or the lure of the desert. As Liechty notes of Kathmandu:

> These contrasting images are a particularly vivid illustration of how the movement of people also involves the movement of places – that is the movement of meanings with which people distinguish separate places within the same space… modern mass tourism intermeshes with modern mass media in the creation of these spatial imaginaries and how 'texts' of many imagined places may occupy a shared spatial 'context' (1996: 112).

Points of Departure

According to Aziz, tourist coastal space in the Sinai is both stable and unstable. Instability arises from the mobile, transient tourist population, but stability is achieved through the 'cultural, ideological and physical structure' of the Bedouins.

> The Coast as a place, possesses its own culture but does not possess its own
> people. The transient-stable nature of the Coast could be compared with that of
> liminality (1999: 174).

It is almost as if modernity is the (external and mobile) cause of instability while
(fixed and internal) tradition is the glue that holds everything together. Ideas
of modernity and heritage keep cropping up in the imagination of the Middle
East – often in binary opposition and therefore in situations of potential conflict
with highly ambiguous Western attitudes. While Egyptian attempts to introduce
modernity find plenty of willing international interest from industries that want
to get the contracts to do the work, such development also clashes with Western
imaginations that want to keep Egypt as a site of heritage alone.

Tensions between these binaries of modernity – and its association with the
West – and its opposite, supposedly represented by the heritage of countries like
Egypt, are not just a symptom of contemporary First–Third World relations. The
bi-directionality of the modernity–heritage, Occident–Orient dualisms could be
seen in Egypt during the colonial period when, says Gregory (2005), the renovation
projects of Mohammed Ali and his son Ismail transformed the area surrounding
the rundown river port of Bulaq into the 'gateway to the Orient'.

> Until the railway from Alexandria to Cairo opened in 1854 this was the usual
> port of entry for European and American visitors to Cairo, who travelled up the
> Nile to Bulaq and then rode east across the floodplain to the city. In the early
> decades it was exceedingly difficult for them to see much of the city from this
> road at all... By the middle of the nineteenth century, the Pasha's twin theatres
> of operation – and 'theatre' is the *mot juste* – had transformed the visual prospect
> of Cairo. The western façade of the city had been aestheticized and its skyline
> dramatically altered. The vista seen by foreign visitors as they disembarked at
> Bulaq was now very different from that of thirty or forty years before. From
> this distance Cairo seemed to present itself as a whole – as a painting in a frame
> – surrounded by lush Oriental gardens that so transported one observer that he
> compared them to 'a garden of paradise'...Cairo was regarded as the epitome of
> an Oriental city (Gregory 2005).

Yet these landscaping projects had been greatly influenced by French ideas of
landscape and garden design and were intended by Mohammed Ali and his son as
symbols of Egypt's embrace of modernity.

Tourist Contact Zones and the Ethnosexual Encounter

Pratt has used the term 'contact zones' to highlight the spatial and temporal aspects of
the practice of colonialism. Contact zones, as opposed to 'colonial frontiers', stress
the 'space of colonial encounters' where 'conquest and domination' took place.

A 'contact' perspective emphasizes how subjects are constituted in and by their relations to each other. It treats the relations among colonizers and colonized, or travellers and 'travelees,' not in terms of separateness or apartheid, but in terms of copresence, interaction, interlocking understandings and practices, often within radically asymmetrical relations of power (1992: 7).

Like the Cairo landscaping of the nineteenth century, 'modern' tourist hotels, bars and clubs of the Sinai, even its desert spaces, are similarly seen as portals of entry both to modernity by Egyptians and to the Orient by tourists.[3] They become 'contact zones' where (like the bodies of the women and the men discussed in the previous chapters) modernity and its 'other' are being constructed into place as well as people. Tourist contact zones might be postcolonial but asymmetrical power relations remain.

The resorts of Sinai might well be gateways to imaginations of different worlds, but as such they allow the participants to 'travel' to these different worlds without actually having to physically leave their own world. It is often assumed, as mentioned previously that 'local' men get involved with tourist women in order to be able to leave their own country and move to the West, particularly in the Middle East. Cohen's (1971) study of 'Arab' boys in Akka, concluded the primary objective of the men's involvement with foreign girls was to get away and leave the country.

As we have seen, for some of the men in the Sinai, moving away from Egypt was their primary objective, even when the women they ended up marrying preferred to remain in the Sinai. Yet many others elected to stay in the Sinai, increasingly aware of the pitfalls of these plans. Many told me how they realised that the hospitality they offered in Egypt would not necessarily be reciprocated if they wanted to return the visit. While we have seen how the privileges of modernity allow people in the West to travel almost anywhere in the world, mobility is far more severely restricted in places like Egypt. If Egyptians want to travel to Europe or North America, they need a visa, but of course tourist visas are not automatically issued at the airport upon arrival, as they are for most European tourists in Egypt. If it is their first application Egyptian nationals have to travel to the relevant Embassy in Cairo and provide a letter of support from a resident of that country stating they will take financial responsibility for them. They also need to prove they have a sufficient amount of money to fund their trip.

With restrictions like this, it is perhaps hardly surprising that marrying a Western woman is considered to be a viable alternative. But while Western media focuses on the threat these men pose as potential immigrants and stereotypes these men as passport chasers, many men do not plan to leave the Sinai after marrying or entering into a relationship with a foreign tourist woman. Amr was a

---

3   The idea of Sinai as a 'portal' where it is possible to move through time was used in the novel *Sinai* (1995) by William Smethurst. Described as a 'time-warp thriller' the hero discovers strange portals on the El Tih plateau where figures from Sinai's past – the Biblical flight of the Israelites from Egypt – are able to enter the present.

wealthy Egyptian who had no difficulty obtaining a visa and could easily travel without financial help from a foreign girlfriend. He had travelled widely in Europe and North America. I asked him what he thought happens to Egyptian men in relationships if they go with their partner to Europe:

> They'll be treated like shit. It's the first time that I feel ashamed to say that I'm Egyptian, when I went to Europe. In Paris and in Italy. I've been treated like shit when I say I'm Egyptian. Really…Since I have been to Italy, I really don't behave the same with Italians, because I know how they treat us there (Amr, 28, Sharm El Sheikh, May 2000).

However, if moving to Europe or North America was considered unattractive for many newly committed couples that came out of these ethnosexual encounters, so too was the idea of moving back to the Cairo suburb or small village in Upper Egypt where their new husband came from. Aside from the lack of work opportunities, the men were generally reluctant to take their bride 'home' except to visit, while the women were too emotionally and imaginatively involved in the meaning-laden Sinai landscape to consider the realities of life in an Egyptian farming village.

In this way many couples opted to remain in the Sinai. Its different history and geographical isolation from long-established Egyptian communities, plus its large tourist resorts and substantial foreigner population meant that the Sinai could be seen to occupy a space between Egypt and the 'West'. The flexibility of tourist space meant it wasn't felt to be necessary to travel to Europe in order to 'escape to modernity'. The landscape of Sinai and the resorts of the Sinai became mediated spaces through which the escape was achieved, without actually having to travel to Europe.

The geographical imagination of the Sinai was as crucial to the men's behaviour there as it was to the women's. In this way the Sinai was imagined, not only as outside of time and place, but also as somehow existing outside of Egypt.

Hassan, 32, was from Cairo originally and worked as a beach DJ in Na'ama Bay. Like many men I interviewed he had first come to Sinai on a holiday himself – visiting friends who worked there. And like many others his plan to stay a few days first by weeks, then by months and then years.

> I didn't know Sharm El Sheikh before but I found it all exciting, a paradise land in Egypt… It was to my eyes a different mentality, because you know when you live in an Arabian country or have the Arabian mentality we have rules and if you are a young boy… because I live in a circle and then when I go out of this circle and see something different, of course I have a surprise… (Hassan, 32, Sharm El Sheikh, May 2000).

Sinai was also a 'paradise' for Egyptian men. This notion of paradise held similar meanings to the notions held by women, but there were also significant differences. For Hassan the 'paradise' meant sun, beaches and palm trees and to some degree local Bedouin culture and ideas of nature and wilderness. However it also included access to what he thought of as European culture and values, instead of stricter Egyptian mores. Paradise included access to modernity, rather than its complete absence. But this modernity was very much viewed as a Western concept, even if it was physically located in Egypt, in Sinai. With the limited mobility (fixity) common to all but the wealthiest Egyptians, the Sinai gave Hassan the opportunity to leave his own community and cultural controls.

Khaled came from a comfortable middle class family and was expected to continue his studies, perhaps by travelling to America. He originally came to work in Sharm El Sheikh as a teenager looking for a holiday job:

> And my uncle said to my mother if your son will go to Sharm El Sheikh, he will never come back. So don't even think about America. I went to Sharm and I didn't come back (Khaled, 28, Sharm El Sheikh, August 2000).

Khaled obviously felt he did not have to travel 'to modernity' in order to experience its freedoms. Like the women from Europe he found the freedom he wanted was available in the Sinai.

> It's my life. Because I love contact with people, I feel free, flying among them, listening to them, England, German, Switzerland, Italians… (Hassan, 32, Sharm El Sheikh, May 2000).

Khaled agreed that this freedom was linked to the freedom to have sex with women but he insisted that wasn't the only attraction.

> I am a boy I cannot say that I don't like girls. But the main attraction is the life here – freedom, sexual freedom, you are free to speak with anyone – life is not complicated like in some parts of Middle East (Khaled, 28, Sharm El Sheikh, August 2000).

European women were not just people to have sex with, but offered him a 'way in' to an imagined modernity and its ideas, something I have discussed in the previous chapter. Relationships with European women offered Khaled and others something that they felt they could not get from Egyptian women, an access to modernity.

> *JJ: Do you think it's easier to talk to European women than Egyptian women?*
> Yes. It's a mentality. European women, they have very easy mentality. Like in the sense if they want to speak about sex or what, speak about politics or what, religion. If you do this with an Egyptian it would be a little bit conservative (Khaled, 28, Sharm El Sheikh, August 2000).

Hassan also spoke of the advantages of a relationship with a European woman in terms of their educational value. These women gave him the opportunity to learn about other cultures and values, without leaving the country:

> You know every day you meet many people from Europe (in Sharm El Sheikh), like England, from Italy, from Switzerland, from Germany. And all each part is thinking about themselves. Like they give you a little mirror about their life. Like we're like this or like that. Look like this, look like that... Before I don't know something like girlfriend and boyfriend, how can I know this? It's not by television because TV is like a movie, but when you speak with the people in reality ... you can give me some experience or some idea about your home, about your culture. What about your work, what about the weather, what about the life there? All of this you can pick it, not by one, by many people, because everybody he can say it like quite the same, so I can trust the people... So I had the imagination from the tourists about this, so this was European culture... (Hassan, 32, Sharm El Sheikh, May 2000).

Hassan and Khaled are articulate, well-educated men from middle class families in Egypt. For men coming from lower socioeconomic backgrounds the impact of Sinai was even more dramatic.

Eid, 28, is from the Sinai and spent his childhood in the backpacker hang-outs in Dahab and Nuweiba so he has become accustomed to the lifestyles of tourists. Over the years he had seen the growing influx of Egyptian men from the Nile Valley coming to work and live in the resorts of Sinai:

> Maybe he's coming from the farmer area. And come to Sinai and just find tourists and different music and all this. And they just see these things only on the TV, and they think that's it, he's out of Egypt (Eid, 28, Dahab, September 2000).

According to Liechty, people in Nepal and the Nepali state see modernity as a foreign commodity, and in so doing, manage to self-peripheralise themselves. As we have seen, the Egyptian men I interviewed in the Sinai have also adopted this perspective by associating all things that are Western, with modern – including Western style clothing and attitudes – mostly from what they have seen in films and what is available through global capitalism. The ubiquitous baseball cap is one example particularly prevalent in the 'modern' Sharm El Sheikh but not uncommon in other parts of the Sinai.

Mills (1996) argues that early feminist work on the relationship between gender and space has tended to focus on the restriction of movement of women in relation to men. However, as we have seen in previous chapters, colonial women's travel, and women's tourist travel in the Third World, has been marked by a sense of freedom both of movement and from gender restrictions. According to Mills the space of the contact zone was highly sexualised and the most 'prominent form of expected contact in these zones was sexual contact or the threat of sexual attack' (1996: 138).

The tourist zones of the Sinai share many of the attributes of colonial 'contact zones'. They are also highly sexualised spaces where, as Pratt notes, 'radically asymmetrical relations of power' between 'travelers and travelees' intersect'. As enclavic regulated spaces however the 'threat of sexual attack', while still present, is somewhat diminished.

By using their Western mobility to actively move from one conceptualisation of place as modern to another pre/un/antimodern place, many women have entered a different 'space'. Imagining a place such as the Sinai in this way, yet also having the feeling of not being 'of the place' has released these women from their normal routine and afforded them greater freedoms. Astrid, 46, from Germany relished the lack of routine available to her in Dahab, where she could follow her whims:

> ...the life here is still very simple. You can concentrate on a thing, you know what I mean. Also you have nothing to do. You don't have to wake up at seven or doing things like this. You eat when you like to eat, you wake up you don't know what the day will bring you – you wake up and you meet this person. You're more open, you...yes you really do what you like to do more (Astrid, 46, Dahab, October 2000).

These freedoms and experimentation with identities that are being experienced are geographically situated within 'tourist zones' that, in turn, play an important in the construction of these geographical imaginations. Tourist places are unique spaces crucial for the performance and experimentation of gender roles/sexual identities for both the men and women, for their interplay and a site where different notions of modernity are negotiated.

It is the acting out of scripts that lends particular meanings to these tourist places. Although the potential for tourist space to offer a performative space that allows experimentation with identity for both tourists and 'locals' is mentioned by Leichty, he argues these 'scripts' 'are often either of commercial origin or are quickly appropriated by commercial interests'.

> ...both visitors and Nepalis share in a middle-class project of mass-mediated dramatization that, while ostensibly uniting groups in a deterritorialized space, ultimately reproduces the structure of global inequality in *re*territorialized spatial imaginaries (1996: 103).

Tourist space plays a crucial role in the negotiations of these tensions and contradictions around the power of gender, race and modernity. Sinai is made up of many different tourist spaces and most of the relationships take place within these spaces.

Within these tourist spaces two different things are happening that are unique to the tourist space. Firstly these Orientalist/Occidentalist fantasies are being instigated and supported by their surroundings of romance and landscape. Secondly these fantasies are being negotiated through space and time (out of modernity's time at least). The Orientalist fantasy is negotiated within notions of gender especially as women experiment with their own gender and sexual identity and the men perform theirs. This is unequal, giving women more freedom – through their economic privilege and mobility – to experiment and call the shots. However this inequality is mitigated by the inequality of global gender relations and is not as extreme as that which the Egyptian man might expect if he was to move to Europe.

Fantasies of the Occident and modernity are also being negotiated. Women might express feelings of antimodernity, but rely on modernity for all their freedoms while their men actively pursue it. The intertwining ambitions and desires of the men and women meet in the establishment of tourist-centred businesses where the men offer authenticity to the tourist experience and the ability to deal with local bureaucratic and governmental controls, while the women bring their greater educational experience and knowledge and ease with modernity's technology to the business, plus their access to clients from their own country. This is not to say that all businesses run this smoothly – there is a lot of deception and fraud – a lot of 'misselling'. Ali, the diving instructor from Dahab was very opinionated about tourist women who got involved with Egyptian men but were later 'ripped off' or just married for their money:

> They follow their heart without thinking. Because sometime his eye come down to the woman, yeah. Come on you are well educated back home. You old enough to know what the fuck is going on. How come you take someone – cannot write his name – a fucking smelly wanker. His shoes, when you get close to him you smell him. What the fuck is going on? So you know the same character if you saw him in the English street you would worried to talk to him. …She should know him first. Does he really want me? Is he really respectable person in his community or is he a wanker. …Is this man, is he really going to be honest with me? I'm Christian, I'm not his culture, I'm open-minded, I'm not a virgin, I am…Do you think this guy is going to be honest with you? Come on this is your mistake, when you lose money it's your mistake…If I respect myself I'm going to respect you. You see me not respecting myself – if I don't have something I cannot give it. If I don't own this cup of tea, I cannot offer it…You can see a guy – he's a very handsome guy. If he went down to where he come from, he's going to get a beautiful wife. But even if he don't want a wife, he's going to get a beautiful chick yeah? But he choose to have a ugly fat fucking woman. For her money. Don't tell me she doesn't know. Bullshit. She knows. She choose this… (Ali, 36, Dahab, October 2000).

The benefits offered through these relationships can be impressive. I met many men who were now fluent in several relationships and had developed IT skills and business skills. Many were involved in small-scale tourism businesses and it is unlikely that they could have found the capital to start up these enterprises without the financial help of the women they met or the international networks created through these relationships. In many ways, these businesses are the glue of the tourism industry in Sinai, providing investment in areas mostly ignored by big business – global and local – and the Egyptian government.

Some examples of the by-products of these relationships include the camps and restaurants in the smaller resorts of Dahab and Nuweiba where women have achieved their dream of 'escape' (for now) by setting up and investing in small businesses catering for tourists and backpackers with their Egyptian or Bedouin partners. These establishments particularly appeal to tourists who are searching for a combination of 'authenticity' and 'modernity' that the tourist imagination has helped to construct as a tourist goal. On the one hand they will find the 'traditional cultural encounter' they have come for, presented as a state of premodernity, but on the other they are assured of comfort and reassurance by a Western standard of practice. Big tourist projects offer modernity, but do not always succeed in the provision of 'authenticity' or the intimacy that so many tourists seek.

Tourist spaces, whether they are enclavic, heterogeneous, translocalities or zones, are spaces which mean many different things to different people; they can be imagined in all sorts of ways and people in them are able to perform a variety of scenarios, not least a romance with a sexualised, racialised other.

Interaction and negotiation within tourist zones allow for the playing out of tensions and potential conflicts between opposing, but also simultaneously occurring, geographical imaginations of leisured space within tourist narratives.

From colonial encounters to contemporary marketing of tourism to Egypt, the region continues to be presented in the West as an ancient and unchanging place – this is what the Western tourist buys and expects to consume.

Egyptian companies and the Egyptian Tourist Board however have adopted a different approach. While they still heavily promote their heritage to tourists, they look to the Dubai business model and prefer to promote the Sinai as an hypermodern space – either from which to visit Egypt's heritage, or as an end in itself with contemporary and luxury beach holiday that can compete with any other Mediterranean or diving resort destination. The stress in promotional literature on the 'ultra-modern' Sinai would seem to suggest that this is an attempt at re-branding the region for Western tourists.

> From Cleopatra's Alexandria to the ultra-modern resorts of Sinai...And just a
> few hours away from Egypt's holiday coastlines is the unforgettable civilisation
> of the pharaohs.

The tourist spaces of the Sinai have become a site where contrasting imaginations of the West and the Orient get played out, nowhere less so than in the resulting ethnosexual relationships between foreign women tourists and local men where the women are looking to Egypt and the Sinai as an escape from modernity, while the men are more likely to be 'negotiating with' – if not actually seeking out – modernity and Western women as representatives of this modernity.

Tourist spaces are places where modernity itself gets defined and where it meets itself in many shapes and forms, where people go to seek modernity and people go to escape it. They are places where roles are changed, identities are experimented with and no matter how 'enclavic' they are, they still allow for a certain level of interaction and negotiating to take place among the different 'players'. Sharm El Sheikh, Nuweiba and Dahab all share elements in common with Liechty's Thamel:

> Thamel is a place with its own distinctive ethos (within Kathmandu), a place in which to pursue a dramatic public lifestyle built around entertainment, leisure, and commercialised/mediated images of sophistication, glamour, and sexuality. Thamel is a quasi-foreign place, a place in which to experiment with, and for those lucky enough, to indulge in images and fantasies of foreignness. Thamel is a place conceptually distinct from 'home' even if 'home' might occupy the same physical space (1996: 102).

The intersecting of gendered power relations with those of cultural difference that occurs within these relationships, within these tourist spaces, does not always reinforce existing power relations. By becoming involved with Western women, local men are able to 'negotiate with modernity' in a way that is not purely colonial or exploitative – as it might be through other male-mediated relationships with the West. The gendered nature of the relationship – and the structures afforded by the institution of marriage for example – can allow them to be, or feel, more in control of this relationship.

As representatives of that modernity – these women are far less threatening to these men than white Western men because of their gender and ambivalent position within the West. After all they can marry and through marriage place these women – and therefore the West – in the potentially subordinate position that the institute of marriage can offer.

Tourist spaces are crucial not only the creation of these encounters, they are also pretty essential to their continuation of any relationships that ensue. Tourist places are unique 'liminal' spaces crucial for the performance and experimentation of gender roles/sexual identities for both the men and women, for their interplay and a site where different notions of modernity are negotiated. Outside of these spaces relationships are subject to different stresses and strains that make the Orientalist/Occidentalist fantasies that underscore these relationships far more difficult to maintain.

Chapter 7
Conclusion

The modern subject…cannot be limited by a narrow focus on the mobility of
traveler or tourist. Rather, modern subjectivity is best conceived in the places of
encounter, where traveler and other meet and are forced to negotiate the meaning
of the place in which they find themselves (Oakes 2003).

In this book I have argued that the postcolonial tourist encounter is not only built
upon and shaped by colonialism and former colonial practice, but that it also
builds upon and reinforces the geographical imaginations contained within these
practices through gender stereotyping and colonial nostalgia.

Said's *Orientalism* (1978) has highlighted the special role of the 'Orient' in the
Western (European) construction of its own identity, while postmodern theorists
have used desert landscapes of tropes of the nomad to explore the concept of modern
subjectivity. However, although these geographical and historical imaginations of the
Orient and its population are heavily gendered, Said tended to avoid the ambiguity
that gender confers in his analysis. Others such as Lewis (1995) and Kabbani (1994)
have highlighted this ambiguity while Mills (1996), McEwan (2000) have explored
the ambivalence created by gender when it cam to Victorian and Edwardian women
travellers and their colonial accounts of the 'other'.

Gender also complicates approaches to the complex question of modern
travel and travel literature. While modern subjectivity and the Euro-Arab
encounter continue to attract the attention of many, as Kaplan (1996) points out,
the subjectivity in question tends to remain a masculine subjectivity, based on a
romantic theorisation of travel, which is prone to succumb to the essentialising
practice of binaried opposites. A gendered approach reveals these inconsistencies
and contradictions, not only in a theoretical or abstract sense in terms of Western
hegenomic notions of femininity and masculinity when directed at 'Eastern'
cultures, but also in terms of how actual men and women behave in their encounters
with 'others'.

When it comes to contemporary Western tourism to Egypt, I have argued that
the women who visit the backpacker camps and beach resorts of the South Sinai
have incorporated geographical and historical imaginations of tropical island
paradise and/or the desert into their imagination of the landscapes and people of
Egypt. However this imagination is not just based on a difference in climate but
a spatial and temporal difference. The Victorian/Edwardian colonial Orientalist
origins of these geographical imaginations mean that a journey to the Sinai is
presented not just as a journey through space, but also time. And it is through these
geographical imaginations that binaries are constructed with the Western cities

and civilisation of modernity on one side and the ancient, traditional nature and wilderness of the Sinai and its people, their supposed opposites, on the other.

Egypt and the Sinai are constructed as an antithesis to modernity, and these imaginations are so prevalent in Western society that travel there is supposed to enable Western tourists to observe 'traditional life' from a distance, and to feel as if they have somehow left modernity.

However, this feeling of distance is not always welcome and a tourist's access to these geographical imaginations can be all too brief, as they can make the experience feel superficial or somehow 'inauthentic'. For many women a romantic and/or sexual encounter with a 'local' man offers the opportunity for a far more enjoyable leisure experience of an othered landscape and people. This is achieved, or at least attempted, because men in the Sinai are also implicated in these geographical imaginations and through racial and sexual stereotyping are seen to embody a form of hypermasculinity, to represent a (pleasing) absence of modernity, and to be inextricably linked to an idea of nature and wilderness that accompany these women's geographical imaginations of (tourist) place.

The idea of a 'transparent space' of the Orient is crucial to these imaginations of the desert for the West. This desire – to escape both from modernity and from oneself – has been a recurring theme and the imagined emptiness of the desert landscape lends itself to this. Yet this empty landscape can only be accessed with the help of local people, revealing the inherent contradictions (and impossibility) of such a construction of place. The journey in mind for the modern tourist is to leave modernity behind when visiting the Sinai resorts and any imagination that does not fit in with expectations of unmodernity causes conflict and tensions, yet of course it is modernity that enables them to do this in the first place.

These relationships are based on many more potential contradictions. The men of the Sinai appeal to the women because they are seen as hypermasculine – based on an Orientalist stereotype of Arab male sexuality. The women I interviewed stressed how their relationships with an Egyptian or Bedouin man made them feel more like a 'woman' than a relationship with a Western man because Arab men were more manly. Yet this masculinity, often based upon the supposedly feminine attribute of sensitivity, was also a heavily restricted masculinity and, because it (mostly) did not apply to their financial or cultural capital, it held little power outside of the relationships.

The position of women who travel from 'modernity' to this tourist space that exists out of time and place changes as a result of this journey. At first glance it seems to offer exciting opportunities for women to experiment with their identity. Yet on closer inspection this new identity might be based on the questionable work of the ethnomasquerade and it probably relies heavily on the status of 'honorary man'; these new 'freedoms' are freedoms of a male subjectivity that originate from mobility and the possession of a greater economic and social wealth than those that are being visited.

In many ways, travelling women are adopting what have been previously been seen to be masculine forms of behaviour and lifestyle – especially those associated with mobility in general and sex tourism in particular. They can also be said to be appropriating mostly masculine colonial geographical imaginations bar the crucial focus on the 'encounter' which can be traced back to Victorian and Edwardian women travellers. Yet these 'masculine' practices are co-opted in order to feel more like 'real women', in order to experience femaleness.

This positioning of the Sinai (and Egypt and the Middle East) as an ancient and timeless place and people positioned on the margins of civilised Europe is constructed through ideas of the Sinai as nature and the desert as an empty marginal space. For tourists the Sinai is a place where anxiety about modernity and nostalgia for pre/unmodernity, where 'antimodernity' can be expressed. The Sinai has become a site for Western women to experience a freedom from modernity. They achieve this by entering into sexual relationships with men who are deemed local and who are seen to embody this condition of un/pre/antimodernity. These women, then, would seem to have incorporated another supposedly male tendency – the desire to escape modernity – which has much in common with modernist discourses of displacement and exile. Like these mostly male theorists, the women tourists have focused on the desert as a site for the expression of this anxiety surrounding modernity. And yet they are using the trappings of modernity – the privileges of life in the West in order to escape it.

But ambivalence remains. These women are not just becoming men. They might be projecting stereotypical images onto the local male population, but they are also incorporating Western stereotypes of the female as 'body' by tanning. Western women might be able to adopt masculine attributes to travel to experience a more satisfying ideal of femaleness in the Sinai, but this is also because they can do so relatively safely; the femaleness is heavily controlled within a framework where the women can hope to stay dominant – or at least increase their power in relation to local men – thanks to their greater economic and cultural capital and the privileges of being Western. And in any case, if it all gets too much they can always get on a plane and leave.

It is the women's mobility, together with their ideas of modernity and its opposites, that allows for experimentation with and reconstituting of, dominant narratives of sexual and other identities of both the female tourist/traveller and the male local.

While performing or 'gender scripting' maleness and femaleness are integral to the relationships between women tourists and their lovers, for many women, these encoutners also offered a means to explore and help to define their own identities. Or, as Beezer (2003) puts it, to reinvigorate their 'jaded Western self' – making the construction of the 'host community' little more than an extension of the construction of the 'local' man as the other.

Male sex tourism is universally condemned and some argue that women who engage in ethnosexual encounters are little different from their male counterparts (SanchezTaylor 2001; Kempadoo 1999, 2001). But just as Victorian and Edwardian women travellers can serve to highlight the ambivalence in colonial practice and help to undermine the essentialisms of Orientalism when gender is ignored, women's sexual encounters can also help to reveal the contradictions contained within the so-called 'sex tourism' so often overlooked when the gender of he person supposedly in power, is also disregarded. Jeffreys (2003) for example, points out the danger of this approach, arguing that it effectively 'degenders prostitution' (2003: 223) and ignores the different 'sex-class positions of men and women'.

> The question of whether women do it too is an important one. It bears on whether it is possible to indict prostitution as an expression of male domination which can be ended, rather than as an inevitable form of human behaviour or just a variety of leisure activity. The insistence that women should be included within the ranks of sex tourists is more than an academic matter. It is one that touches on the whole way in which international systems of prostitution should be understood and addressed (2003: 238).

In *Heading South* (dir. Laurant Cantet 2005: also known as *Vers La Sud*) set in the 1970s, middle-aged women travel to Haiti and give native boys presents in exchange for sex. So far, so like men. However the way these relationships get played out over the course of the film show the complexity of gender, race and class involved, in a way that male sex tourism would struggle to reveal. So are these ethnosexual encounters better described as romance tourism instead? Are women in the Sinai who become involved with local men, testing 'the constraints of conventional gender identity present in Western culture'? (Pruitt and LaFont 1995: 435) Well, they are certainly looking for – and finding – a relationship where they are more in control, and where the rewriting of the 'gender script' involves borrowing some traits normally associated with masculinity. For example, their adoption of the position of the modern travelling subject, their First-World status with its accompanying economic and cultural capital *and* their mobility expressed in their freedom to travel freely back and forth between the two different spaces – the space of modernity in Europe from whence they obtain their privileged position and the (geographically imagined) space of the unmodern, premodern and antimodern Sinai where they exhibit their privileges and where their privileges become exaggerated and worth more in the local currency.

Their mobilised imagination of place takes the women to a different space where their own society's rules of sexual behaviour do not need to be adhered to.

A concept of 'romance' can be useful when looking at these relationships but only in the context of the construction of travel as a romantic engagement with the past, an emotional attachment to an imagined geography of place and people. Perhaps it can also be used in reference to a particular discourse, a narrative that Western women use – particularly when conversing with researchers from the West – to describe, rationalise and ultimately justify these relationships. After all, activities like instigating sexual relationships, paying for sex, changing partners several times in one week, sleeping with a man half your age, taking a younger lover when you are in your mid-sixties is common practice among some women tourists in the Sinai. Yet they are – still – not deemed normal female behaviour in the West, while 'falling in love', and becoming emotionally involved most definitely are.[1]

These women challenge other notions of acceptable femaleness by actively seeking out these relationships. They are often instigating relationships and experimenting with their identity as women within the relationship as they find themselves to be the person in the traditional role of the man with greater mobility cultural capital and economic power.

By becoming involved with Western women, local men can 'negotiate with modernity' in a way that is not purely colonial or exploitative – a way that leaves them feeling in control, to some extent, of the relationship with the West. As representatives of that modernity women are far less threatening to these men than white Western men because of their gender and ambivalent positionality. After all, these men can marry these women, and marriage can help them to engage with the women – and to some extent with Western modernity – in a potentially more powerful position.

The men in these relationships have also been influenced by the dominating geographical imagination that places them at the margins, on the periphery of modernity and Europe and the West in the centre. Women in the West are seen to embody Western values and represent modernity. And, just as the women see a relationship with a local man as a gateway to another existence, of antimodernity, the men often see these women as approachable (and encroachable) gatekeepers to modernity.

Engaging in relationships, including marriage, with these women can therefore be a means of interacting with the West in a far less confrontational and purely exploitative manner than through a more direct experience of globalised neoliberal capital or its predecessor, colonialism.

Again the relationship between modernity and the Sinai is a complex one. There are many different modernities. While many women associate the Sinai with these antimodernities, most Egyptians and Bedouins see the Sinai, especially Sharm El Sheikh, as very much representing modernity in the Middle East.

While the label 'real men' is used to refer to Egyptians and Bedouins, the wilderness and landscape of the Sinai is a crucial location for this masculinity. We have seen that such was the image and appeal of Bedouin men to women tourists that it wasn't uncommon for Egyptians to deliberately pass themselves off as Bedouins in order to fulfil women's desires for a gendered racial sexual fantasy of the Arab masculinity.

Egyptian and Bedouin men can be seen to be exhibiting Occidental geographical imaginations by incorporating Orientalist stereotypes into their behaviour with women and mixing in a few of their own stereotypes about European women. But

---

1 It could perhaps be argued that women's sexual encounters on holiday are impacting on their behaviour when at home as it is becoming increasingly common for older women to enter in relationships with younger men, so much so that a new term 'cougars and cubs' has been coined to describe it.

while they have adopted certain stereotypes surrounding masculinity that incorporate the women's geographical imaginations, they do not imagine the Sinai or themselves as 'premodern', 'unmodern' and 'antimodern' in the same way as the women. The stereotypes are used because they are thought to work in their favour and use imaginations of the desert and the beach that support this gendered identity.

As we have seen ideas of modernity and tradition keep cropping up in the imagination of the Middle East – often in binary opposition and therefore in situations of potential conflict with highly ambiguous Western attitudes.

Sinai's particular history and geographical isolation from long-established Egyptian communities, plus its large tourist resorts and substantial foreigner population, means that it is often not imagined as fully Egypt by many Egyptians. For many Egyptians a trip to Sharm El Sheikh is like a visit to a fantasy theme park of Western sensibilities combined with 'local' atmosphere; it is an adventure into a Western lifestyle. Yet for European visitors it is supposed to be – among other things – the Orient in all its splendour, the wonders of the Red Sea and the lure of the desert. It is imagined as 'modern' by the men at the same time as it is being imagined as 'ancient' by the women.

While Egyptian men (and to some extent Bedouin men) admire and aspire to the modernity of Sharm El Sheikh, the 'modernity' of the enclavic tourist resort was so unattractive to some of the tourists that anything would be done to avoid these places, rhetorically at least. But they are also 'portals' and their gateway status means in practice they are hard to avoid – it is here you will find the physical as well as symbolic entry and exit points, the apparatus of travel in the form of airports and bus stations, taxis. The concentration of technologies in modern tourist space means that they are usually required at some point by all travellers, as mobility requires constant attention if it is to be maintained.

Modern tourist space is a contemporary necessity if Western women are to travel, even though it might simultaneously be blamed for destroying the illusion it works so hard to create. After all, an empty desert is not really that alluring – without these men, and their historicised masculinity, the desert would become a feminised, impoverished landscape, with limited accessibility, stripped of its ability to take these women to another place and time.

Landscapes of longing need tourist spaces because tourist spaces and the people who work in them can offer a myriad of meanings and modernities to both local and visitor. Moreover they continue to do so despite, or because of, their glaring inconsistencies and the intuitive impossibility of being so many different times and spaces. Interaction and negotiation within these points of contact allow for the playing out of tensions and potential conflicts between opposing but simultaneously occurring geographical imaginations. Tourist spaces are places where 'modernity' meets itself in many shapes and forms, where people go to seek modernity and people go to escape it. They are places of possibility where roles are changed and identities are experimented with. Yet tourist space remains inherently unstable, and the ability of changes within tourist space to impact outside their gendered temporalities are much harder to access.

Bibliography

Ahmed, S. 1998. Tanning the Body: Skin, Colour and Gender. *New Formations* No. 34, Summer, 27–42.

Albuquerque, K.D. 1998. Sex, beach boys and female tourists in the Caribbean. *Sexuality and Culture* 2, 87–111.

Alloula, M. 1986. *The Colonial Harem*. Trans. W. Godzich. Minnesota: University of Minnesota Press.

Appleyard, D. http://www.dailymail.co.uk/femail/article-561156/Sun-sand-sex-stupidity-Why-thousands-middle-aged-women-obsessed-holiday-gigolos.html.

Aziz, H. 1999. Negotiating Boundaries and Reconstructing Landscapes: A Study of the Relations between Bedouin, Tourists and the State. PhD Thesis, University of Surrey.

Bach, E. 1997. Sheik Fantasies: Orientalism and Feminine Desire in the Desert Romance. *Hecate* 23, 9–40.

Baudrillard, J. 1988. *America*. Trans. C. Turner. London: Verso.

Bauman, Z. 1996. From Pilgrim to Tourist – or, A Short History of Identity. In S. Hall and P. du Gay (eds), *Questions of Cultural Identity*. London: Sage, pp. 18–36.

Bauman, Z. 1997. The Making and Unmaking of Strangers. In *Debating Cultural Hybridity: Multi-cultural Identities and the Politics of Anti-Racism*. London: Zed Books.

Beezer, A. 1993. Women and Adventure Travel. *New Formations* 21, 119–30.

Beezer, A. 2003. Negative Dialectics of the Desert Crash in *The English Patient*. In J. Arthurs and I. Grant (eds), *Crash Cultures: Modernity, Mediation and the Material*. Bristol, Portland: Intellect Books, pp. 131–42.

Behbehanian, L. 2000. Policing the Illicit Peripheries of Egypt's Tourism Industry. *Middle East Report* 216, 32–4.

Bell, G. 1939. *The Letters of Gertrude Bell Vol. 2*. London: Pelican.

Bell, G. 2001. *The Desert and the Sown: The Syrian Adventures of the Female Lawrence of Arabia*. New York: Cooper Square Press.

Bell, C. 2005. Tourism as Colonial Nostalgia. *Africa Quarterly* 45, 64–7.

Bernal, M. 1991. *Black Athena: The Afroasiatic Roots of Classical Civilization*. London: Vintage.

Bernstein, M. and Studlar, G. 1997. *Visions of the East: Orientalism in Film*. New Brunswick: Rutgers University Press.

Bhabha, H. 1994. *The Location of Culture*. London: Routledge.

Birkett, D. 1989. *Spinsters Abroad: Victorian Lady Explorers*. Oxford: Basil Blackwell.
Blunt, A. 1994. *Travel, Gender and Imperialism: Mary Kingsley and West Africa*. New York and London: The Guilford Press.
Boissevain, J. 1989. Tourism as anti-structure. *Kultur Anthropologisch* 30: 145–9.
Bondi, L., Davidson, J. and Smith, M. 2005. *Emotional Geographies*. Aldershot: Ashgate.
Boone, J. 1995. Vacation Cruises, Or, the Homoerotics of Orientalism. *Publications of the Modern Language Association* 110, 89–107.
Bourdieu, P. 1986. The Forms of Capital. In John Richardson (ed.), *Handbook of Theory and Research for the Sociology of Education*. New York: Greenwood Press, pp. 241–58.
Bowman, G. 1996. Passion, Power and Politics in a Palestinian Tourist Market. In T. Selwyn (ed.) *The Tourist Image: Myths and Myth Making in Tourism*. London and New York: John Wiley and Sons Ltd, pp. 83–103.
Bryman, A. 1988. *Quantity and Quality in Social Research*. Contemporary Social Research: 18, Series editor: M. Bulmer. London: Unwin Hyman.
Clifford, J. 1997. *Routes: Travel and Translation in the Late Twentieth Century*. Cambridge, MA: Harvard University Press.
Cohen, E. 1971. Arab boys and tourist girls in a mixed Jewish–Arab community. *International Journal of Comparative Sociology* 12, 17–33.
Croutier, A.L. 1998. *Harem: The World Behind the Veil*. New York: Abbeville Press.
Dahles, H. and Bras, K. 1999. Entrepreneurs in Romance Tourism in Indonesia. *Annals of Tourism Research* 26, 267–93.
Davies, M. and Jansz, N. 1999. *Women Travel: Adventures, Advice and Experience* Harrap. Book review in *New Statesman and Society*.
Dobie, M. 2001. *Foreign Bodies: Gender, Language and Culture in French Orientalism*. Stanford: Stanford University Press.
Ebron, P. 1997. Traffic in Men. In M. Grosz-Ngate and O. Kokole (eds), *Gendered Encounters: Challenging Cultural Boundaries and Social Hierarchies in Africa*. New York: Routledge, pp. 223–44.
Edensor, T. 1998. *Tourists at the Taj: Performance and Meaning at a Symbolic Site*. London and New York: Routledge.
El-Gawhary, K. 1995. Sex Tourism in Cairo. *Middle East Report* 196, 26–7.
Fabian, J. 2002. *Time and the Other: How Anthropology Makes its Subject*. New York: Columbia University Press.
Frankenberg, R. 1993. *White Women, Race Matters: The Social Construction of Whiteness*. London: Routledge.
Frohlick, S. 2005. Romance and adventure, sex and surfing: Allure of 'the tropics' on the Caribbean coast of Costa Rica. Paper presented at American Association of Geographers conference, 5–9 April, Denver, Colorado.

Frohlick, S. 2007. Fluid Exchanges: The Negotiation of Intimacy between Tourist Women and Local Men in a Transnational Town in Caribbean Costa Rica. *City and Society* 19, 139–68.

Frow, J. 1991. Tourism and the Semiotics of Nostalgia. *October*, Vol. 57 pp. 123–57.

Garber, M. 1992. *Vested Interests: Cross-Dressing and Cultural Anxiety.* New York: Routledge.

Garcia-Ramon, M-D., Albet-Mas, A., Nogue-Font, J., and Riudor-Gorgas, L. 1998. Voices from the Margins: Gendered Images of 'Otherness' in Colonial Morocco. *Gender, Place and Culture* 5, 229–40.

Geniesse, J. 2001. *Passionate Nomad: The Life of Freya Stark.* New York: Modern Library.

Ghassoub, M. and Sinclair-Webb, E. 2006. *Imagined Masculinities: Male Identity and Culture in the Modern Middle East.* London: Saqi Books.

Glaser, M. 1978. *Sinai and the Red Sea.* Tel Aviv: Steimatzky.

Gregory, D. 1994. *Geographical Imaginations.* Cambridge, MA and Oxford: Blackwell.

Gregory, D. 1999. Scripting Egypt: Orientalism and the Cultures of Travel. In J. Duncan and D. Gregory (eds), *Writes of Passage: Reading Travel Writing.* London: Routledge, pp. 114–50.

Gregory, D. 2001. Colonial Nostalgia and Cultures of Travel: Spaces of Constructed Visibility in Egypt. In AlSayyad, N. (ed.), *Consuming Tradition, Manufacturing Heritage: Global Norms and Urban Forms in the Age of Tourism.* London and New York: Routledge, pp. 111–51.

Gregory, D. 2005 Performing Cairo: Orientalism and the City of the Arabian Nights. In N. Al-Sayyad, I. Bierman and N. Rabat (eds), *Making Cairo Medieval.* Lanham MD: Lexington Books/Rowman and Littlefield, pp. 69–93.

Grewal, I. 1996. *Home and Harem: Nation, Gender, Empire and the Cultures of Travel.* Durham, NC and London: Duke University Press.

Hackforth-Jones, J. and Roberts, M. (eds), 2005. *Edges of Empire: Orientalism and Visual Culture.* Wiley Blackwell.

Hall, S. 1997. The Spectacle of the Other. In S. Hall (ed.) *Representation: Cultural Representations and Signifying Practices.* London: Sage Publications in association with the Open University.

Hammersley, M. 1990. *Reading Ethnographic Research: A Critical Guide.* London: Longman.

Herold, E., Garcia, R. and DeMoya, T. 2001. Female Tourists and Beachboys: Romance or Sex Tourism? *Annals of Tourism Research* 28, 978–97.

Hopwood, D. 2000. *Sexual Encounters in the Middle East.* London: Ithaca Press.

Jacobs, J. 2003. The Literature on Sex Tourism and Women Negotiating Tourism in the Sinai. PhD dissertation, Open University.

Jones III, J.P., Nast, H.J. and Roberts, S. 1997. *Thresholds in Feminist Geography: Difference, Methodology, and Representation.* Lanham MD: Rowman and Littlefield.

Judd, D.R. 1999. Constructing the Tourist Bubble. In D.R. Judd and S.S. Fainstein (eds), *The Tourist City.* New Haven and London: Yale University Press.

Kabbani, R. 1994. *Imperial Fictions: Europe's Myths of Orient.* London and New York: Rivers Oram Press/Pandora.

Kandyoti, D. 1991. *Women, Islam and the State.* London: Macmillan.

Kaplan, C. 1996. *Questions of Travel: Postmodern Discourses of Displacement.* Durham, NC and London: Duke University Press.

Kaur, R. and Hutnyk, J. (eds), 1999. *Travel Worlds: Journeys in Contemporary Cultural Politics.* London and New York: Zed Books.

Kholoussy, H. 2004. Stolen husbands, foreign wives: Mixed marriage, identity formation, and gender in colonial Egypt, 1909–1923. *Hawwa: Journal of Women of the Middle East and the Islamic World* 1, 206–40.

Konuk, K. 2004. Ethnomasquerade in Ottoman–European encounters: reenacting Lady Mary Wortley Montagu. *Criticism*, Summer 2004. http://findarticles.com/p/articles/mi_m2220/is_3_46/ai_n15954410/ Wayne State University Press.

Lavie, S. 1990. *The Poetics of Military Occupation: Mzeina Allegories of Bedouin Identity under Israeli and Egyptian Rule.* Berkeley, CA and Oxford: University of California Press.

Lewis, R. 1995. *Gendering Orientalism: Race, Femininity and Representation.* London and New York: Routledge.

Lewis, R. 2003. On Veiling, Vision and Voyage: Cross-cultural Dressing and Narratives of Identity. In S. Mills and R. Lewis (eds), *Feminist Postcolonial Theory: A Reader.* New York: Routledge, p. 536.

Liechty, M. 1996. Kathmandu as Translocality: Multiple Places in a Nepali Space. In P. Yaeger (ed.) *Geographies of Identity.* Ann Arbor: University of Michigan Press.

Lindqvist, S. 2000. *Desert Divers.* Trans. Joan Tate. London: Granta Books.

Littlewood, I. 2001. *Sultry Climates: Travel and Sex since the Grand Tour.* London: John Murray.

Löfgren, O. 1999. *On Holiday: A History of Vacationing.* Berkeley, CA and Oxford: University of California Press.

Lorius, C. 1997. 'Desire and the Gaze': Spectacular Bodies in Cairene Elite Weddings, *Women Studies International Forum* 19(5) September–October.

MacCannell, D. 1973. 'Staged authenticity: on arrangements of social space in tourist settings' *American Journal of Sociology* 79: 589–603.

MacCannell, D. 1984. 'Reconstructed ethnicity: tourism and cultural identity in third world communities' *Annals of Tourism Research* 11, 361–77.

MacCannell, D. 1992. *Empty Meeting Grounds: The Tourist Papers.* London and New York: Routledge.

MacCannell, D. 1999. *The Tourist: A New Theory of the Leisure Class.* Berkeley, CA: University of California Press.

Mårdh, P.-A., Arvidson, M. and Hellberg, D. 1997. Casual travel sex, sex tourism and international prostitution. *Travel Medicine International* 15(4).

Massad, J. 2007. *Desiring Arabs.* Chicago: University of Chicago Press.

Massey, D. 2005. *For Space*. London, Thousand Oaks and New Delhi: Sage.

Mathy, J-P. 1993. *Extreme-Occident: French Intellectuals and America*. Chicago: University of Chicago Press.

McCarthy, J. 1994. *Are Sweet Dreams Made of This? Tourism in Bali and Eastern Indonesia*. Indonesia Resources and Information Program, Northcote Vic, 19–20.

McClintock, A. 1995. *Imperial Leather: Race, Gender and Sexuality in the Colonial Contest*. London and New York: Routledge.

McClintock, A. 2001. *Double Crossings: Madness, Sexuality and Imperialism*. Vancouver: Ronsdale Press.

McEwan, C. 2000. *Gender, Geography and Empire: Victorian Women Travellers in West Africa*. Aldershot: Ashgate.

Meisch, L.A. 1995. Gringas and Otavalenos: Changing Tourist Relations. *Annals of Tourism Research* 22, 441–62.

Melman, B. 1992. *Women's Orients: English Women and the Middle East, 1718–1918, Sexuality, Religion and Work*. Ann Arbor: University of Michigan Press.

Mills, S. 1991. *Discourses of Difference: An Analysis of Women's Travel Writing and Colonialism*. London and New York: Routledge.

Mills, S. 1996. Gender and Colonial Space. *Gender, Place and Culture* 3, 125–47.

Minca, C. and Oakes, T. 2006. *Travels in Paradox: Remapping Tourism*. Lanham MD: Rowman and Littlefield.

Mitchell, T. 1988 *Colonising Egypt*. Cambridge University Press.

Moghadam, V.M. 2003. *Modernizing Women: Gender and Social Change in the Middle East*. Second Edition. Boulder, CO: Lynne Rienner Publishers.

Momsen, J.H. 1994. Tourism, gender and development in the Caribbean. In V. Kinnaird and D. Hall (eds) *Tourism: A Gender Analysis*. London and New York: John Wiley and Sons.

Moss, M. and Moss, G. 1987. *Handbook for Women Travellers*. London: Piatkus.

Moss, M. 1999. You want to be a woman alone, but are you safe? *The Observer* Travel Advice 24 January pp. 6–7.

Moss, P. 2002. *Feminist Geography in Practice: Research and Methods*. Oxford: Blackwell.

Mulvey, L. 1975. Visual Pleasure and Narrative Cinema, *Screen Magazine* 16(3): 6–18.

Nagel, J. 2003. *Race, Ethnicity, and Sexuality: Intimate Intersections, Forbidden Frontiers*. New York: Oxford University Press.

Oakes, T. 2005. Tourism and the Modern Subject: Placing the Encounter between Tourist and Other. In C. Cartier and A. Lew (eds), *Seductions of Place*. London and New York: Routledge.

O'Connell Davidson, J. and Layder. D. 1994. *Methods, Sex and Madness*. London: Routledge.

O'Connell Davidson, J. and Sanchez Taylor, J. 1999. Fantasy Islands: Exploring the Demand for Sex Tourism. In K. Kempadoo (ed.) *Sun, Sex and Gold: Tourism and Sex Work in the Caribbean*. Lanham MD: Rowman and Littlefield, 37–54.

Osborne, P.D. 1990. Milton Friedman's Smile: Travel and Culture and the Poetics of a City, *New Formations* Summer – Subjects in Space No. 11.

Pasztory, E. 2001. Nostalgia for Mud. In *The Pari Journal* [The quarterly publication of the Pre-Colombian Art Research Institute] 11(1) Winter.

Peleggi, M. 2005. Consuming colonial nostalgia: The monumentalisation of historic hotels in urban South-East Asia. *Asia Pacific Viewpoint* 46, 255–65.

Pels, D. 1999. Privileged Nomads: On the Strangeness of Intellectuals and the Intellectuality of Strangers. *Theory, Culture and Society* 16: 63–86.

Phillips, J.L. 1999. Tourist-oriented prostitution in Barbados: the case of the beach boy and the white female tourist. In K. Kempadoo (ed.), *Sun, Sex and Gold – Tourism and Sex Work in the Caribbean*. Lanham MD: Rowman and Littlefield, 183–200.

Pollock, G. 1994. Territories of Desire: Reconsiderations of an African Childhood Dedicated to a Woman Whose Name was Not Really 'Julia'. In G. Robertson, M. Mash, L.Tickner, J. Bird, B. Curtis and T. Putnam (eds), *Traveller's Tales: Narratives of Home and Displacement*. London and New York: Routledge, 63–92.

Pratt, M.L. 1992. *Imperial Eyes: Travel Writing and Transculturation*. London: Routledge.

Pruitt, D. and LaFont, S. 1995. For Love and Money: Romance Tourism in Jamaica. *Annals of Tourism Research* 22(2): 422–40.

Rojek, C. and Urry, J. 1997. Transformations of Travel and Theory. In C. Rojek and J. Urry (eds), *Touring Cultures: Transformations of Travel and Theory*. London and New York: Routledge.

Rosaldo, R. 1993. Imperialist Nostalgia. In *Culture and Truth: The Remaking of Social Analysis*. London: Routledge.

Russell, M. 1988. *The Blessings of a Good Thick Skirt: Women Travellers and their World*. London: Collins.

Ryan, C. and Hall, M.C. 2001. *Sex Tourism: Marginal People and Liminalities*. London and New York: Routledge.

Said, E.W. 1978. *Orientalism: Western Conceptions of the Orient*. London and New York: Routledge.

Sanchez Taylor, J. 2000. Tourism and 'embodied' Commodities: Sex Tourism in the Caribbean. In S. Clift and S. Carter (eds), *Tourism and Sex: Culture, Commerce and Coercion*. London and New York: Pinter.

Sanchez Taylor, J. 2001. Dollars are a Girl's Best Friend? Female Tourists' Sexual Behaviour in the Caribbean. *Sociology* 35(3): 749–64.

Selwyn, T. (ed.) 1996. *The Tourist Image: Myths and Myth Making in Tourism*. London and New York: John Wiley and Sons.

Sieg, K. 1996. Ethno-Maskerade: Identitatsstrategien zwischen Multikultur und Nationalismus im deutschen Theater. *Frauen in der Literaturwissenschaft Rundbrief* 49, December: 20.

Silverman, K. 1992. *Male Subjectivity at the Margins*. New York: Routledge.

Soueif, A. 1999. *The Map of Love*. London: Bloomsbury.

Stark F. 1982. *The Southern Gates of Arabia: A Journey in the Hadramaut*. New York: Modern Library.

Stevenson, C.B. 1982. Female Anger and African Politics. In *Turn of the Century Women 2, Part 1*, 7–17.

Stoler, A.L. 1995. *Race and the Education of Desire: Foucault's History of Sexuality and the Colonial Order of Things*. Durham, NC: Duke University Press.

Tomlinson, J. 1991. *Cultural Imperialism*. London: Pinter Publishers.

Urry, J. 1990. *The Tourist Gaze*. London: Sage.

Urry, J. 1995. *Consuming Places*. London: Routledge.

Urry, J. 2001. Globalising the Tourist Gaze, published by the Department of Sociology, Lancaster University at: http://www.comp.lancs.ac.uk/sociology/soc079ju.html.

Veijola, S. 2006. Heimat Tourism in the Countryside: Paradoxical Sojourns to Self and Place. In C. Minca and T. Oakes (eds), *Travels in Paradox: Remapping Tourism*. Lanham, MD: Rowman and Littlefield.

Wagner, U. 1977. Out of Time and Place: Mass Tourism and Charter Trips. *Ethnos* 42: 38–52.

Wallach, J. 2005. *Desert Queen: The Extraordinary Life of Gertrude Bell: Adventurer, Adviser to Kings, Ally of Lawrence of Arabia*. New York: Anchor Books.

Wilson, R. 1994. Goodbye Paradise: Global/localism, Hawaii and Cultural Production in the American Pacific. *New Formations* 24, 35–50.

World Tourism Organization Market Intelligence and Promotion Department 2005 *Tourism in Egypt and the Sharm el-Sheikh attack: First Special Report on the impact of the Sharm el-Sheikh attack*. Madrid 11 August.

Wynn, L. 2007. Women, Gender and Tourism: Egypt. In S. Joseph (ed.) *The Encyclopedia of Women and Islamic Cultures, Vol. IV: Economics, Education, Mobility, and Space*. Leiden: Brill.

Yegenoglu, M. 1998. *Colonial Fantasies: Towards a Feminist Reading of Orientalism*. Cambridge: Cambridge University Press.

Yuval-Davis, N. 1997. *Gender and Nation*. London: Sage.

Index

For Product Safety Concerns and Information please contact our
EU representative GPSR@taylorandfrancis.com, Taylor & Francis
Verlag GmbH, Kaufingerstraße 24, 80331 München, Germany